I0434664

SOUNDS OF SIRENS

SOUNDS OF SIRENS

◆

Essays in African Politics & Culture

Kwame Okoampa-Ahoofe, Jr.

iUniverse, Inc.
New York Lincoln Shanghai

SOUNDS OF SIRENS
Essays in African Politics & Culture

iUniverse, Inc.

For information address:
iUniverse, Inc.
2021 Pine Lake Road, Suite 100
Lincoln, NE 68512
www.iuniverse.com

LCCN: 2004110575

ISBN: 0-595-32678-1

Printed in the United States of America

I dedicate this collection to the eternal memory of my father, Professor Kwame Okoampa-Ahoofe, Sr., (1929–2001), who often admonished me to stop worrying too much about the seemingly intractable socioeconomic and political woes of Africa, a salutary admonishment of which I was never quite apt to heeding.

Also, to the unquenchable spirits of Dr. Kwame Nkrumah, Jomo Kenyatta, Patrice Lumumba, Walter Sisulu, Walter Rodney, Samora Machel, Amilcar Cabral, and the epic continental African struggle for intellectual, cultural, socio-political and economic freedom.

And my maternal elder cousin, Samuel Kwadwo Adu, a former West African table-tennis champion, whose harrowing experiences in Ghana partly inspired the title of this volume.

Contents

Acknowledgments

I am grateful to the following relatives, friends and colleagues who, among a legion of others, have been very encouraging of my literary efforts over the years: Dmitry Urnov, Margaret Agyemang Duah, Rev. Professor Kofi Asare Opoku, Abu Shardow Abarry, Charles Owusu, Ralph Nazareth, Norman Spencer, Rosette Finneran, Bruce Urquhart, Roberta Kramer, Sammy Browne, Eric K. Baning, Marian Parish, Anthony Techie-Mensah, Nathaniel Norment, Abena Aninwaa Okoampa-Ahoofe, Dolly Doris Nyanyo Mensah (aka Mama Afua Oye), Adwoa Apeakoramaa Okoampa-Ahoofe, Willie K. Egyir, Alex Kabba, Paul Doyle, Roger Gocking and Martin Larbi.

Introduction

Sounds of Sirens constitutes the first of a projected ten-volume collection of my journalistic writings and book reviews, among other things, over the past sixteen years and counting. Such writings, which have been largely spontaneous and avocational, have appeared in such notable diasporic and continental African newspapers and journals as the ***New York Amsterdam News***, where I almost single-handedly and single-mindedly made book reviews a regular ***columnar*** activity for nearly five years, until the editor-publisher of that historic African-American societal and cultural fixture bluntly confided to me that the art of book reviewing, or literary criticism, was accorded the lowest priority by the ***Amsterdam News***; and also that my style of writing was rather too outlandish and cognitive—she had actually used the term ***intellectual***—for the type of audience which the paper primarily served. I had obstinately pointed out to the editor-publisher that the book-selling business was a major cottage industry, particularly in the predominantly African-American Harlem, where the headquarters of the ***Amsterdam News*** are located, and within the New York metropolitan area's vast African-American community at large. Unfortunately, such mild and polite protestation came to naught, as I soon began picking some of my ***well-sweated*** submissions from waste-paper baskets and abandoned bookshelves in the third-floor editorial suite of that august publication. I decided then and there that that proverbial revelatory moment had arrived for me to pick up the broken pieces, as it were, lick my badly contused ego and move on.

It is interesting and significant to, herein, observe that the preceding scenario was more strikingly general or common than isolated or personal. For, during the course of the fifteen years that I freelanced for the ***New York Amsterdam News***, legions of the finest writers and sacrificial journalists ever produced by the Black community were forced by untoward ideological and, on occasion, personal circumstances to strike set or decamp. And almost all of these highly professional people have gone on to very successful and remunerative careers, where they have reportedly been properly appreciated and supported.

So it seems, perhaps not without good reason or cause, on the part of its proprietors, that the ***Amsterdam News*** has determined its role to be primarily that of a seminal training ground for prospective giants and luminaries of the larger media industry. Needless to say, that legendary weekly has definitely served in such capacity or fashion for the author, and he is unreservedly grateful for the opportunity to have written for the *Amsterdam News* and almost fanatically and religiously served the African-American community.

Among the publications in which some of the essays and articles herein collected have appeared is the *African Monthly*, a rather wistfully short-lived Houston, Texas-based journal on whose editorial board the author enthusiastically served; also *African Profiles International*, of which he served as deputy editor from 1990–1992. And the *Nigerian News Digest*, now defunct and later published under the more inclusive and expansive name of *African News Weekly*, out of Asheville, North Carolina.

Presently, the author serves as a columnist and occasional editorialist for the freely circulated bi-weekly newspaper *African Abroad*, easily the foremost publication on African Affairs here in the United States. He also serves as a leading opinion columnist and occasional reporter for the *New York Beacon*, perhaps the most widely circulated and read African-American weekly in the New York metropolis and its environs.

During the course of the last sixteen years that he has been seriously engaged in *service journalism*, as he prefers to characterize it, the author has published some four-hundred pieces, ranging across all journalistic genres—i.e. news reports, book, theater and movie reviews, political commentary and sports. And during the last five years, he has regularly taught journalism courses at Nassau Community College of the State University of New York at Garden City. Such spirited academic engagement has convinced him of the indispensable need of actively participating in the training of the next crop or generation of opinion shapers here in the United States and elsewhere.

The overriding motivation for assembling this collection of essays and articles has been the popular request of readers, some of whom earlier expressed their regret for having lost track of "your highly informative and well-composed" pieces over the years. This group of readers thus originally expressed their desire in having a comprehensive collection of my essays, as well as other writings, in book form, for personal reading enjoyment, as well as pass on copies to relatives, friends and associates; and also keep on their shelves.

Generally, the essays and articles herein collected reflect my deep-seated interest and perspectives on continental African political history and culture. They are unabashedly aimed at modestly influencing major policy-makers in directions that the author, rather presumptuously, deems to be the most salutary and propitious for the collective development of the African continent, in general, but more particularly the global Black community. In a real sense, therefore, this anthology may be deemed as the modest contribution of the proverbial ***African Abroad***, a native son in sojourn (geographically speaking) who never quite left the primeval continent (both psychologically and culturally).

Sincerely,
Kwame Okoampa-Ahoofe, Jr.
Bronx, New York
June 25, 2003

1

Ghana's Independence: A New Meaning

There is a running joke in Ghana that when you hear the wailing siren of an ambulance, it is most likely a dead body being conveyed to the hospital. For in modern Ghanaian parlance, hospitals have become virtual morgues. I am also told that it is more lucrative for ambulances to carry corpses than live-human cargo, because those who often get critically ill before calling for medical assistance these days are the poorest of the poor.

This brings us to a sorry-ass article that appeared in the Internet version of **The Ghanaian Chronicle** of December 15, 1999. This newspaper lead-article matter-of-factly reported that: "Doctors and nurses on duty at the Mamprobi Polyclinic, Accra, on December 7 abandoned their patients to celebrate the 50th birthday of a colleague."

If, indeed, the preceding sounds callous to the sensitive reader, obviously the concerned reader may be either foreign to the country or out-of-touch with events in the proverbial motherland. For this sorry state of affairs very much reflects what has come to be identified with the Ghanaian national temperament in the post-colonial era; actually what has come to characterize Ghanaian ethos in the neo-colonial era. It is indubitably symptomatic of the pseudo-civilian Ghanaian government, which after having butchered, summarily executed, liquidated and stampeded virtually every able-bodied citizen into thoughtless cowardliness or outright exile, has for the past 19 years emulated, with inimitable finesse, the very sins and crimes for which other equally detestable rulers (or is it mis-rulers?), such as Generals Akuffo and Acheampong, were summarily executed by firing squad.

Whoever invented the epochal concept of "Millennium" gave the doctors and nurses of Mamprobi Polyclinic a prime weapon to literally "doctor" their patients. And here again, it is worth noting that these days in Ghana being a

1

"Patient" simply means the primary English definition of the word: The religious "capacity to endure hardship, difficulty, or inconvenience without complaint" (*American Heritage College Dictionary 3 rd Edition*).

Thus the article, written by Emmanuel Akli, goes on to observe: "It all began at exactly 11am when a nursing mother returned from Consulting Room 2 with a message for her *colleague patients* that she had been asked by a Dr. Komaxo to wait outside because the doctor was going to celebrate his 50th birthday, dubbed 'Millennium Birthday Party.'"

I emphasize the phrase "colleague patients" not for any linguistic or dictional reasons, but simply to draw attention to the grim fact, on the threshold of the twenty-first century, that the tragic irony of the Ghanaian public health system these days is that oftentimes patients are more "collegial" or functionally professional than their rather aristocratic providers. Thus when one hears the groaning sirens of an ambulance, what one may actually be hearing are the disconsolate grouse of patients complaining about the curious fact that healthcare practitioners are either wantonly mal-practicing, or they are simply gloating over the problems of their patients, problems which they are paid to either help resolve or meliorate. It is doubtful whether Dr. Komaxo's so-called Millennium Birthday Party had any redeeming effect on his patients, short of aggravating their collective pain and suffering. And it is almost certain that we will never know the extent to which Dr. Komaxo's "Millennium Birthday Party" celebration contributed to the premature deaths or permanent injury of his patients. "Within a moment," we are further told, "all the doctors and nurses at the polytechnic [sic] had gathered at Consulting Room 4 corking up champagne while others stood outside, pop-eyed with excitement, as their colleagues enjoyed their champagne, singing birthday songs on top of their voices."

What sticks in my craw more than anything else, is the apparent precipitous dearth of respect and decorum in Mr. Rawlings' Ghana. Emmanuel Akli's story continues: "The reporter was an eye-witness to the whole drama and saw an elderly man who could not believe what was happening walk to the entrance of the consulting room and draw the attention of one of the nurses to the large number of patients waiting to be attended to. But the old man drew the ire of the revelers and insults were rained on him, forcing him to quietly leave the place."

Needless to say, even when one commonsensically acknowledges the fact that most Ghanaian doctors are quite conscientious and diligent, in spite of the government's apparent lukewarm support for the public health system, it cannot be gainsaid that a national professional ethics panel, or perhaps even an institute, is in dire demand. Indeed, some of the patients who attended the Mamprobi Polyclinic on December 7, 1999, recognized such need, as Mr. Akli further noted: "Some of the patients, mostly women, who could not control their temper, rushed on the free-boozing doctors and nurses and hooted at them for their unethical behavior, but [eve] that did not deter them from the merry-making. Instead, one of the nurses came out angrily and told the patients that those who could not wait could go to Korle-Bu [the central hospital of Accra and Ghana] for prompt attention. The party lasted for about an hour before normal consultation [resumed]."

Your guess is as good as mine, on the question of whether party-giddy doctors and nurses could perform up to the optimum standards of their practice, let alone improve. The irony is that the putatively ramshackle state of the Ghanaian public health system has often been attributed to a lack of foreign exchange resources, rather than common sense and a respectful professional attitude towards the proverbial Hippocratic Oath. In Ghana, these days, the strident sound of an ambulance frantically racing through the streets of Accra and Kumasi may be of no consequence at all; indeed, any siren sound in Ghanaian cities, these days, may yet be announcing the heady and lordly celebration of a Dr. Komaxo's "Millennium" birthday bash.

2

Harvest of Foolery

On May 20, 1998, when I landed at Ghana's main and, to-date, only international airport in the capital city of Accra, something foreboding—in the Nietzschean sense—hit me right in the face. The occasion was the mournful conveyance and interment of the mortal remains of my mother, who had passed right here in New York City two months before. The foreboding phenomenon had to do with the look of the airport; nothing about the airport had constructively changed during the 13 years that I had sojourned abroad. Which, in this case, is not to echo the proverbial dictum that: "The more things change, the more they remain the same." For the seeming lack of any appreciable change, in this instance, glaringly emphasized the purely diplomatic, if also euphemistic, designation of Ghana and other countries with similar sociopolitical and economic status as "developing countries." Indeed, in this instance, one could not agree more with that rather trenchant critic who poignantly described most countries in the West African sub-region as "progressively under-developing countries."

By the time I left Accra Airport on June 20, after having spent a month in the country, Ghanaian and other air-travelers still had to be ferried by buses from the main terminal building across the tarmac into their respective carriers. How nothing had changed in 41-years of post-colonial governance, I cursed under my breath. Forget about the fact that to-date the Accra Airport has no lounge for relatives and friends seeing off and welcoming travelers; I soon gathered from the grapevine that such abject lack was a security measure aimed at stanching drug-trafficking, or some such anti-social racket. The eyesore result were the myriad of teeming societal undesirables—beggars, con-artists and plain-faced muggers—relentlessly milling in front of the building.

This is not to say that the country is averse to any form of modernization. Not even when one takes stock of the fact that in at least 27 (now 29) of the 41 (at the time of this revision 43) years of post-colonial Ghana, and still counting, the "benign" military dictators who run the country have consistently demonstrated

4

their inordinate penchant for stockpiling ammunition in the purported defense of some chimerical organism called "national security." And here, it is significantly instructive to observe that none of the myriad putsches and coup detats have been staged by any other than bona fide members of the Ghanaian military. Granted, some rascal civilians are known to have staunchly backed such regressively Darwinian means of political access, including a world-renowned Oxford University-educated former prime minister. Interestingly, in July 1956, when President Nkrumah's Convention People's Party (CPP) won a landslide electoral victory, Dr. Kofi Abrefa Busia rode herd on a delegation to the British colonial office in London, to petition the British Crown, and Ghana's extant colonial overlord, to desist from granting the already-scheduled return of Ghana to self-governance. Fortunately, Dr. Kofi Abrefa Busia and his right-wing bourgeois reactionaries did not succeed. He would, however, succeed ten years later in backing the military junta that unseated the Nkrumah administration and facilitated the precipitous devolution of Ghanaian national destiny.

Indeed, it is interesting to observe that Ghana's major and, to-date, only international airport is named for General E.K. Kotoka, the very Darwinian outlaw who spearheaded the grossly unimaginative overthrow of the constitutionally elected government of the CPP. For many detractors and outright enemies of Nkrumah, Kotoka's greatest—if also sole—achievement was simply getting rid of an elected dictator. It has often been said, largely by Western academics and critics, that Nkrumah was a heartless and fatuous dictator; these days, one hears Mr. Jerry John Rawlings, the career soldier who ran Ghana for twenty harrowing and incontrovertibly bloody years, described as a "benign dictator." It is significant to observe that Mr. Rawlings, whose agnatic parentage is purported to be Scottish, presided over the dastardly kidnapping and summary execution of three Ghanaian supreme court judges, all of whom belonged to a single ethnic nationality.

When one agrees with the Western ideological mythology that Nkrumah was a raw-boned dictator bereft of vision, then it begins to make sense that General Kotoka's statue should continue to command the august façade of the Accra International Airport, thus perpetually humiliating those of us who incurably believe in democratic governance. Needless to say, the 1966 Kotoka-led coup initiated the barbaric, neo-colonial military dynasty that Ghanaians continue to suffer under such bizarre guises as the National Liberation Council (NLC), Supreme Military Council (SMC), Armed Forces Revolutionary Council (AFRC), National Defense Council (NDC), National Commission for Democracy (NCD) and, of course, the pseudo-constitutionally appointed and substantive National Democratic Congress (NDC),

That Ghana's post-colonial political dilemma transcends military dictatorship cannot be honestly gainsaid. In fact, many of the most vociferous civilian opposition party leaders, some of whom are currently sitting in parliament, representing misguided and hoodwinked constituents, are known to have collaborated with Kotoka's so-called National Liberation Council to unseat President Nkrumah. It is also significant to observe that these largely superannuated rascals and executive national, fiduciary muggers continue to dominate whatever passes by the name of "the legitimate opposition." This state of affairs, coupled with a largely under-educated and under-informed electorate, has made it almost impossible to rectify the prevailing socioeconomic chaos ravaging the country.

These days, a high school graduate has to forcibly endure at least a two-year waiting period before gaining admittance into one of the country's three full-fledged universities and the two bogus or largely nominal and political point-scoring universities. It, therefore, came as no surprise to me, albeit rather appalling, to observe (when I visited the country two years ago) that more than half of all children of school-going-age were out on the streets peddling dog-chains, toilet tissues, watch straps, bread and cookies and barely readable newspapers. The sad aspect of this tragic story is that nobody in the top-echelons of government seems to be worried about the kind of intellectual and cultural sheaves that Ghanaians are wont to be harvesting another generation from now.

Matters are no less meliorated or indemnified by the progressively lurid working conditions accorded Ghanaian public school teachers. At the time of this writing (March 2000), almost all the major Ghanaian newspapers are bemoaning the fact that legions of teachers in many parts of the country have yet to draw a month's salary in nearly twenty-four months! Even the conservative government-run *Daily Graphic* observed in its on-line editorial page of December 12, 1999, that "It is baffling that hundreds of teachers, some of whom have sacrificed to teach in deprived and disadvantaged areas of the country, would go without pay for as long as 15 uninterrupted months." Further, the conservative government mouthpiece added that: "The Director-General of the Ghana Education Service (GES), Professor Christopher Ameyaw Akumfi, is reported to have issued an assurance to such trained teachers that their salaries and arrears would be paid by the end of this month." Indeed, one hardly needs a college degree, much less a doctorate, to arrive at the frightful but pragmatic conclusion that Ghana's national security is in woeful jeopardy. This desolate state of affairs has been minted by a government that ushered itself into power with the sanctimonious slogan of "Probity and Accountability," as well as orchestrating the brutal murder of judges and ordinary citizens.

The English writer George Orwell is quoted as having observed that: "The [human] imagination, like certain wild animals, cannot breed in captivity." Needless to say, the same analogy could be made in reference to the collective Ghanaian national vision. One only has to take a cursory look at the media, particularly those of the print sector, to arrive at such acute conclusion. Indeed, the Ghanaian media may be aptly said to be suffering from a "Crisis of Grammar." A recent news-article which appeared in the on-line edition of *The Ghanaian Chronicle* (December 15, 1999) had the following curious title: "Critics Want *to Deprives* Us of Benefits of *Chimps* Project." What is perplexing about the preceding is the fact that in spite of the Internet's typographical flexibility, for as long as the aforementioned article was posted, the editors did not see any good reason to correct the title. The article itself, however, was quite edifying, even if it also reflected the lingering neo-colonial mentality of many contemporary Ghanaians, particularly those in the economically strapped rural principalities. It opened thusly: The chiefs of the Nkonya Ntumda area in the Jasikan District of the Volta Region where the chimps from the U.S. are to be settled, have condemned organisations and individuals calling for a halt to the chimpanzee project, saying it will deny them the benefits to be derived from the project...."

To-date, I know of no Ghanaian region which has adopted chimps as a staple diet. Of course, the great diversity of human tastes and sensibilities prompts me to suspect the veritable existence of a chimp-chomping "brotherhood" in our midst. Fortunately, however, that was not quite the point of the chiefs of Nkonya Ntumda. No, they were "convinced," among other things, that "the project would provide jobs for the youth and boost tourism in the area." In the wrenching throes of hunger, a fatal canker, to be sure, the leaders of Nkonya Ntumda had determined that the "zoologization" of their region by "American-born chimps of African descent" was worth the risk of their miserable lives. Perhaps these chiefs should have invited their janitorial and chamber-pot-toting peers in these United States to come down to Nkonya Ntumda and give them the lowdown, as it were, on America's socioeconomic goodwill towards the global African community. Ultimately, it seems, sanity has prevailed, with Mr. Rawlings calling for "a probe into the project until all the health and environmental concerns have been addressed by the various stakeholders." Indeed, there is a deficiency in the grammar of thought, in addition to idiomatic grammar. And a "probe" is often best interpreted as a tactical hold-off until such a time that most of the potential and prospective victims have become amnesiac. That the Nkonya Ntumda chiefs should predicate their acceptance of the "chimpanzeenization" of their lands and forestry resources on a documentary film screened by the American group Friends of Animals (FOA), is quite enlightening coming on the threshold of the twenty-first century.

It was, however, the opinion piece by Kwadwo Darko-Sekyi, titled "Twenty Long Wasted Years of (P)NDC Rule" (**Chronicle** 12/15/99), which convinced me that the government of Chairman Rawlings, indeed, ought to be arraigned before a Nuremberg-type tribunal to account for the gross cognitive dissonance of the bulk of what these days passes for enlightened popular discourse. In his bid to aptly demonizing the regime of the so-called National Democratic Congress, Darko-Sekyi also fatuously attempts to hagiographize the Acheampong-Akuffo junta of total political decadence and abject national moral temperament. Thus, regarding the June 4, 1979 "revolution," the writer gushes: "It was the fateful day on which certain miscreants arrogating to themselves the appellation of leaders rose against the nation and against the consciousness of society, against those born and yet unborn, against all that is decent in humanity and declared an atavistic onslaught on all that is good in Ghana." Really, it is this kind of "Ananse-literature" that stands to do us more harm as a polity than the temporally transient, albeit unacceptable, atrocities of Mr. Rawlings and his kleptocratic posse. For the very dignified existence of any people devolves on a vigilant and honest preservation of memory. Darko-Sekyi's approach to popular history, it is interesting to note, veritably reflects a blistering deficiency in both cognitive and idiomatic grammar. Of course, there are no idiots in the land of my birth and ancestry, except angry pen-pushers who are so angry that the truth, where it seems to even tangentially favor their enemies, becomes the very enemy of truth, which in effect amounts to retrospective hyperbole, a rather curious sort of relativist-revisionism.

3

Nobody Lives Here Anymore

For many of his detractors, Ghanaian president Jerry John Rawlings is a veritable cut of the same ideological cloth as late Nigerian dictator General Sani Abacha. Whether such accusation, characterization or assessment has any semblance with objective reality may be deemed moot. Nevertheless, to these detractors, Rawlings' stopover in Abuja, the Nigerian capital, on his return trip from the summit of the Organization of African Unity (OAU) in Ouagadougou, the Burkinabe capital, in June 1998, vindicated their insistent claim beyond the proverbial reasonable doubt.

The symbolic significance of Rawlings' Nigerian stopover, with several top members of his cabinet, including the chief of the armed forces and some members of the Council of State, the Ghanaian equivalent of the British House of Lords, might have been two-fold: to condole with the Abacha family and any other Nigerians who felt bereft of the notorious dictator's hitherto imperious presence, as well as to assure the unstinted goodwill of Ghana to the citizens of Africa's most populous nation.

The latter gesture might have become necessary in view of the fact that shortly before Abacha's death (in June 1998), the Nigerian government had released a statement accusing Ghana of covertly scheming for the overthrow of the late dictator. In the past, similar complaints, accusations and allegations had been leveled against the (P)NDC regime of Mr. Rawlings. In the preceding instance, however, the Nigerians were alluding to a just-concluded United States-sponsored conference on human rights in Ghana—a clearly ironic venue—during which General Abacha's widely perceived political intransigence had been among the major topics discussed. Needless to say, many Ghanaians who did seem to quite appreciate the belligerent import of the Nigerian complaint were measurably disturbed, including the moderator—or spiritual leader—of the Presbyterian Church of Ghana, who promptly paid a courtesy call on the president in order to seek official clarification. As was to be expected, Mr. Rawlings vehemently denied that any such scheme or plot existed, and further expressed his regret that the Nigerian government would choose to hold a press conference on the matter without having first conferred with the latter's Ghanaian counterpart. Of course, nobody could blame Mr. Rawlings for eerily recalling that the last time leaders of Nigeria's major ethnic groups—notably the Ibos and the Hausas—started accusing each other of calculated ill-will, an excess of five million Nigerians of all professional shades and ideological leanings paid dearly with their lives.

The preceding notwithstanding, flying into Abuja with his topmost henchmen, simply to condole with Nigerians over what was widely deemed to be a providential poetic justice for Abacha, did not amuse many Ghanaians. Neither did most Nigerians seem to deem such gesture to be expressly one of goodwill. In Ghana, for instance, several newscasters and radio personalities swamped the airwaves with congratulatory messages for the people of Nigeria on the seemingly auspicious demise of "Mobutu's twin-brother." One such eloquent speaker was the popular Gabby Adjetey of JOY-FM, arguably Ghana's most powerful, privately-owned radio station. In a presentation which very much echoed Mark Antony's in Shakespeare's *Julius Caesar*, Adjetey prayed that Africa would never have to suffer a reprise or reincarnation of the likes of Abacha, Bokassa, Mobutu, Doe and Idi Amin.

Indeed, it is not quite certain whether the Ghanaian premier appreciated both the symbolic and moral implications of flying into the Nigerian capital. Either Mr. Rawlings, having wielded both stratocratic and elective power for 16 years (up to 1998), had understandably and woefully lost touch with the ordinary citizenry of the two countries, or he had simply assumed that these two peoples were possessed of a temporally stunted sense of moral justice. On the other hand, if indeed Mr. Rawlings genuinely believed that both Ghanaians and Nigerians envisaged Abacha to be an accurate representation of democratic ideals and aspirations, then we are deep trouble!

That the Ghana of President Rawlings's National Democratic Congress (NDC) is grossly out of touch with reality is amply borne out by the ramshackle state of all levels of education. Recently, the country's Committee of Vice-Chancellors and Principals of tertiary institutions issued a statement indicting the government for intellectual and cultural negligence (see *The Independent* 8/10/99: 1,12). In parts, the statement highlighted the fact that: "some local employers and international organizations have questioned the quality of products [i.e. graduates] of the country's universities." Already, the British education ministry, the very administrative establishment that formulated and supervised most of modern Ghana's academic curriculum in the colonial era, and continues to exert significant influence on our post-independence educational system, has report-edly been re-examining the coordinate meritorial recognition of the Ghanaian academy. This is largely due to the widely perceived decline in the quality of the country's hitherto internationally respected academic and professional caliber. The Committee of Vice-Chancellors has warned that unless reconstructive resources are forthcoming from the NDC government, to ensure the necessary maintenance of our hitherto globally celebrated high academic standards, current enrollment of freshmen would have to be halted, in addition to "dis-admitting" at least 30-percent of freshmen currently enrolled in the three major Ghanaian universities.

What is rankling for many a well-meaning Ghanaian, both at home and abroad, is the seemingly inordinate rash of members of Mr. Rawlings' cabinet, as well as other top government officials and civil servants to dispatch their children, relatives and wards abroad, mainly to the United States and Europe, for a per-ceived better quality of education, even as the government vehemently denies that academic standards at the nation's'major higher educational institutions have dramatically declined. President Rawlings' eldest daughter, Ezanator, has been reportedly shipped out of the country for tertiary studies in the United States; some even claim Ezanator is either in Holland or Switzerland (*The Inde-pendent* 8/10/99: 1). It goes without saying that any highly-placed public official who has no vested interest in fortunes of the country's educational system cannot be reasonably expected to efficiently supervise the system, much less be envisaged as an admirable role-model.

Many more government officials who are known to have sent their children and wards abroad for further studies, among them Professor Kofi Awoonor, former dean at the University of Cape Coast; Dr. Christine Amoako-Nuamah, former minister of education and currently minister of Lands and Forestry Resources; Mr. Victor Selormey, minister of Finance, who is known to have three children studying abroad; Mr. Daniel Ohene Agyekum, a quondam diplomat and current Greater Accra regional minister; Mr. Simon Abingya, deputy minis-ter of Mines and Energy; and Mr. Richard Dornu Nartey, of the ministry of Lands and Forestry Resources—the list goes on and on.

In the late 1980s, this writer had a heated confrontation with Mr. James Vic-tor Gbeho, then-Ghana's permanent representative to the United Nations, and currently the minister in charge of Foreign Affairs. The dispute hinged on Mr. Gbeho's denial of any existence of inter-ethnic dissension in the country, on the specious grounds that the European missionary-minted boarding school system fostered a curious breed of multiculturalism that ensured that academic and professional merit, rather than "tribalism" regulated the sphere of socioeconomic relations. Nearly 12 years later, this writer still insists that the public and administrative spheres of Ghanaian life are highly tribalized, and that the least constructive mode of resolution is via pat and glib public denials, such as that which Mr. Gbeho indulged during the celebration of one of Ghana's independence anniversaries. Interestingly, at the aforementioned forum, held at the New York City Technical College, in Brooklyn New York, Mr. Gbeho dared this writer to return immediately to Ghana and throw in his lot as part of a purported, on-going national reconstruction exercise, in order to vindicate my stance as a well-meaning and patriotic Ghanaian. Of course, I was quite amused at the proposition, in view of the fact that Ambassador Gbeho's children were widely known to be schooling at elite Mid-Western institutions, and elsewhere in the United States. Indeed, it is such unmitigable arrogance that makes some Ghanaian public officials believe in their civic sanctity and democratic self-will, even while magisterially denying others whom they deem to be "lesser Ghanaians," that may be deemed to constitute the crux of the country's post-independence leadership dilemma.

In the final analysis, the salutary possibility of studying abroad may be deemed the least of our developmental woe—indeed, the foremost contributors to the socio-cultural and economic development of Ghana in both the colonial and post-colonial eras, were largely trained in institutions of higher learning abroad. Among them are the immortalized President Kwame Nkrumah, Dr. J.B.(K.K.) Danquah, Mr. William Ofori-Atta, and Dr. K.A. Busia. The difference between the times of Kwame Nkrumah and his peers and our generation, however, is that in our time the facilities for quality higher education at home exist. If these facilities are inadequate, it is largely due to administrative mis-management and untold political corruption. To be certain, many of the top-members of the so-called National Democratic Congress (NDC) obtained their first degrees from Ghanaian universities—among these are Professor Kofi Awoonor, Dr. Ibrahim Chambas, Dr. Mohamed Ben Abdallah and Mr. Vincent Assiseh.

Not very long ago (1998?), President Jerry John Rawlings sat on ABC-TV's "Like It Is," an African-American community affairs program, and straight-facedly told the host, Mr. Gil Noble, that the NDC government was unique in Ghana's political annals because unlike, implicitly, the CPP and subsequent governments, no member of Mr. Rawlings's cabinet had children, relatives and wards studying abroad who were being sponsored by these public officials. Now we know that Mr. Rawlings is a bold-faced liar; not that we haven't been aware of this seamy aspect of the Ghanaian potentate all along. In recent times, it has even been whispered under the grapevine that the President has bought a mansion in Houston, Texas, next to the residence of Nigerian-American basketball legend Hakeem Olajuwon, where Mr. Rawlings' children and other kin regularly vacation. It is interesting to recall that for most of his tenure as a military dictator and subsequently as a pseudo-elected president, Mr. Rawlings has castigated the United States and its Western Allies for their gross expropriation and exploitation of Africans and their resources. And while one may not quibble with the fact that human beings mature and change, it is hardly acceptable for a leader who predicated his political raison detre on "probity and accountability" to brazenly chart a morally degenerate mode of governance, even as Mr. Rawlings continues to vaunt his relative ideological moral probity. Ghanaians have not forgotten, and are not likely any time soon to forget Mr. Rawlings' summary executions of renowned and unknown citizens in the name of "House Cleaning." Recently, the President was reported to have apologized for the extra-judicial excesses of the AFRC/ PNDC eras amidst cheers of the predominantly NDC "Amen Corner" in the Ghanaian parliament. This is not the first time that Mr. Rawlings has apologized for his flagitious deeds; neither do we expect the January 2000 parliamentary apology to be his last. It is almost certain that his children and grandchildren would live to regret in perpetuity, for having been unfortunate enough to be born to such a morally un-redeemable terrorist. Paradoxically, however, Mr. Rawlings may, after all, not be without any redeeming features. His wanton atrocities and dastardly and unprincipled leadership have almost ensured that most Ghanaians are not likely to forget the bitter fruits of his tenure any time soon. And while no well-meaning Ghanaian should crave his unworthy blood, Mr. Rawlings, nevertheless, must not be allowed to go quietly into the proverbial sunset. He must be made to stand trial for his gross public misconduct, unless, of course, like Chile's General Pinochet, Mr. Rawlings is medically certified to be psychologically incompetent. The era of providential vengeance through Pentecostal paroxysm, should be forever and squarely consigned to history.

Mr. Rawlings' legacy to the chaotic landscape of West African politics, in particular, and African politics in general, might also be aptly seen in the abject legacy of Nigeria's General Sani Abacha. Indeed, recently Nobel literature laureate Professor Wole Soyinka, who has been known to have staunchly supported the Ghanaian president through most of his reign of terror, accused Mr. Rawlings of having accepted $5million of Nigerian public funds from General Sani Abacha, in order to facelift the latter before Western governments (see *Asenta* February 2000). Mr. Soyinka has issued a debt collector's call to the Ghanaian leader, who has roundly characterized the former's allegation as preposterous. For Mr. Rawlings to have willingly shilled for Mr. Abacha, as the celebrated Nigerian artist and scholar alleges, implies that the Ghanaian president saw Mr. Abacha as his mirror-image, or in Eliot-ian terms his *doppelganger*. And this, as intellectually insulting as it sounds to both Mr. Rawlings and some of his Ghanaian admirers and lackeys, might not, indeed, seem all that curious, once it is amply understood that like his more politically advanced counterpart, General Abacha had actually intended to civilianize himself in order to "democratically" hand over power to President Abacha. And this is exactly what the arguably astute Ghanaian strongman did in 1992, when having browbeaten and pistol-whipped his countrymen and women for nearly 11 years, Flt.-Lt. Rawlings handed over elective power to President Rawlings. Indeed, all that Mr. Rawlings had done then was to delete the letter "P" of his PNDC (or Provisional National Defense Council) government and come up with the more catchy and poetic NDC (or National Democratic Congress). Paradoxically, the leaders of the opposition who prided themselves in being far better educated and more politically savvy than Mr. Rawlings, their purported high school dunce, as well as his henchmen, were leaping over each other conjuring such dippy and hardly memorable names as People's National Convention, National Convention Party and People's Convention Party. This was in their frantic, if also addled, attempt at retaining whatever cynosure remained of President Nkrumah's Convention People's Party. Rawlings, ever the mercurial political chameleon, had out-maneuvered the opposition by insisting that no new parties be created using the exact names of any of Ghana's pioneering political parties. Of course, Chairman Rawlings had not imposed any poetically stultifying restraint on his own political imagination. In the process, the best name that the most serious challenger to the NDC could conjure was the rather 29th—centuryesque New Patriotic Party.

On July 15, 1998, a front-page *New York Times* news-report, which also carried his picture, quoted former Nigerian president General Olusegun Obasanjo—the only African military ruler to have handed over power to a civilian government without recidivizing or relapsing—as saying that General Abacha was more than an evil personality, and that the late dictator had been pronounced clinically insane. Interestingly, like Mr. Rawlings but in a quite oblique manner, General Obasanjo has now become the elected President Obasanjo of Nigeria. The preceding notwithstanding, one wonders whether such a tyrant and world-renowned butcher, as General Sani Abacha, deserves a condoling stopover by the president of a country which projects itself as a democratic paragon and paradigm for the West African sub-region.

4

In Celebration of Nothingness

In his philosophical, classic treatise titled ***The Myth of Sisyphus*** (1955), French North-African thinker and Nobel Literature Prizewinner Albert Camus observes: "Beginning to think is beginning to be undermined." Indeed, this sentiment can be clearly seen to underlie the attitude of Ghana's ruling National Democratic Congress (NDC) towards the bulk of that nation's citizenry. Apparently, and alarmingly, aware that not many Ghanaians agree that the NDC has achieved anything of substance in the 16 years (up to 1998) that it has wielded power, the government has recently resorted to a fitful celebration of whatever it deems to be among its most sterling achievements. One such milestone celebration, which was raucously observed while I was in the country recently (May-June, 1998), was the so-called June 4th Anniversary. It marked the first time that Flt.-Lt. Jerry John Rawlings, now the constitutionally elected president of Ghana, took up arms and, in one fell swoop, wiped out the entire leadership of the then-ruling military junta in 1979—the so-called Supreme Military Council (SMC). Needless to recall, this sanguinary move was hitherto unprecedented.

The reason for such emotionally traumatizing action, according to the protagonist, was "to clean house" and ensure the strict maintenance of "probity and accountability" among the national leadership. Rawlings also stated that the June 4th Uprising, as it shortly thereafter came to be known, was undertaken to restore constitutional democracy, a proclamation that he studiously followed by handing over power to the civilian government of the late Dr. Hilla Limann. Barely two years later, Rawlings would stage another coup to undermine the very constitutional government whose fundamental tenets he claimed to staunchly uphold.

On December 31, 1981, when he re-took power and summarily abolished the so-called Third Republic of Ghana, Mr. Rawlings set up what he called his Provisional National Defense Council (PNDC), another supposedly temporary measure aimed at momentarily restoring "genuine democracy." At that time, the substantive Ghanaian president accused Dr. Limann of running the country socio-economically aground. The *cedi* (Ghana's monetary currency) had been unimaginatively devalued, and Rawlings claimed that not only had the prices of food items and other so-called essential commodities skyrocketed, but that the Limann government was the most disgraceful administration in the country's history. What, in fact, Flt.-Lt. Rawlings had done during the three months that he ran the country before handing over power to Dr. Limann, was freeze the prices of general merchandise well below viable market prices; needless to recall, Ghana did not produce most of such merchandise. Thus, Limann took over a ramshackle economy which could only be resuscitated by implementing a free-market strategy. Indeed, it was during the admittedly trying process of revamping the country's economy that Rawlings came in for the seeking time, and has since retained power. [At the time of this revision, March 2000, Mr. Rawlings, reportedly, was preparing to permanently exit the political scene, at least as president, as stipulated by the so-called Fourth Republican Constitution of Ghana].

The June 1979 uprising, therefore, was nothing more than the grossly misguided, albeit well-intentioned, action initiated by a group of low-ranked military officers who seemed to firmly believe that their senior colleagues were abusing both the inviolable trust and socioeconomic destiny of Ghanaians. Among the legion leaders summarily executed during the above-mentioned uprising, were General Ignatius Kutu Acheampong, shortly before his execution stripped of his military rank and veteran's status, and who ruled Ghana from 1972 to 1978; General F.W.K. Akuffo, who had unseated General Acheampong via a palace coup and, whom Flt.-Lt. Rawlings directly deposed—incidentally, the success of Rawlings's coup is often blamed on General Akuffo's purported megalomania; General A.A. Afrifa, the young upstart who is credited, along with Generals E.K. Kotoka and A.N. Ankrah, for overthrowing President Kwame Nkrumah; Air Vice- Marshall Yaw Boakye; Colonel R.E.A. Felli; and Commander Utuka.

In 1983, three Ghanaian Supreme Court justices, all of whom belonged to the same ethnic nationality, were kidnapped from their homes in the thick of the night and executed Mafia-style. A dastardly attempt to burn their bodies beyond recognition, however, failed when it rained heavily on the Greater-Accra Plains shortly after the victims had been set alight. Subsequent investigations by Ghanaian law-enforcement agents and patrician legal experts indicated that a top, inner-circle member of Flt.-Lt. Rawlings' Provisional National Defense Council had, indeed, authorized and also supervised the gang-style execution of Mrs. Justice Koranteng-Addow, then in an advanced stage of pregnancy, and Justices Agyepong and Sarkodie. A retired senior military officer and former managing director of the Ghana Industrial Holdings Corporation (GIHOC), Major Sam

Acquah, was also executed along with the above judges. Later, Mr. Joachim Ama-rtey-Kwei, the ranking PNDC member who allegedly ordered the executions, and who was one of a handful of civilian members of the PNDC cabinet, would be sentenced to death by firing squad and swiftly dispatched, following a vehe-ment national outcry. The names of other top officials of the PNDC were also suggested in connection with the brutal execution of the Supreme Court judges; however, nothing substantive came of it. In fact, most members of a Special Investigations Board (SIB) that presided over the inquest which the government initiated had to flee the country, after receiving anonymous letters threatening their lives. One of the investigators, a former dean of the University of Ghana's School of Law, who fled the country in fear of his life, today teaches at Temple University in Philadelphia.

To-date, none of the numerous buildings and other significant national insti-tutions and landmarks which Mr. Rawlings's government has been fitfully re-naming for supposedly distinguished Ghanaians and other Africans bear the names of any of the assassinated judges. It is interesting to observe, however, that even notorious military dictators like Captain Thomas Sankara, of Burkina Faso, have monuments named for them; in the case of the late Burkinabe strongman, a roundabout or circle in the Ghanaian capital of Accra bears his name. The gov-ernment of the National Democratic Congress has until now demonstrated no remarkable passion for judicial integrity by, for instance, celebrating the lives of those intrepid judges whose sole crime was to have conscientiously upheld the very laws and constitution of the land which the (P)NDC claims to be its sole source of political legitimacy. Indeed, it cannot be honestly gainsaid that the murdered judges are more deserving of a national holiday, rather than observing the parliamentarily rubber-stamped celebration of June 4th, the commemoration of a veritably undemocratic putsch. Here in America, we have something called "jury nullification," a relatively benign form of judicial travesty; in Ghana and most of Africa, what we have may be aptly called "jurist liquidation." Maybe by legislating June 4th as a national holiday, the NDC government is hoping that Ghanaians would soon forget to think, so as not to undermine the former's legit-imacy.

Then, once again, in Camusian terms, there is the otherwise risible, if it were not so dauntingly tragic and embarrassing, case of Nigeria where indigenous thought seems to have been opprobriously replaced by something called "reli-gious conflict." Recently, a front-page article appeared in the ***New York Times*** titled: "New Strife Tests Nigeria's Fragile Democracy" (March 15, 2000). What is striking about the preceding headline is its creative vapidity. For, "strife" is not a new phenomenon to post-colonial Nigeria, and neither is "fragile democracy." In other words, but for the sake of reportage of momentous events that is the essence of good journalism, nothing in the above-referenced bulletin, written by a Norimitsu Onishi, merited our sedulous attention. The latter observation because the writer, whom one may reasonably assume to be of Japanese descent, does not demonstrate any appreciable comprehension of Nigeria's political historiography. Therefore, what Mr. Onishi (or is it Ms. Onishi?) ends up with, by the designation of "news," is a melange of quotations from obviously, genuinely frustrated Nigerians who want the chronic Islamo-Christian warring to cease forthwith.

That the country continues to celebrate something called "Independence," whose 40th anniversary Nigerians will be marking come October, with all pomp and circumstance, beggars the moral imagination. But it is also quite understandable for the people of a country whose hangover, or even love-affair, with the salutary departure of the crassly exploitative British colonialist seems to override all other national considerations.

The recent Kaduna riots, in which to-date 400 people, all "religious adherents," are officially known to have perished, has almost become pedestrian to those of us who have studiously followed the anfractuous fortunes of the proverbial giant of Africa. In about 1989 or 1990, similar "religious riots," largely between people describing themselves as "Muslim" and "Christian," left hundreds of thousands dead in their wake. What makes the problem quite a conundrum is the fact that in Nigeria it is often unclear where ethnocentrism differentiates itself against religionism, especially when any ideological collision between these often ends in raw carnage and an abject state of terror, the Q'uran and the Bible notwithstanding.

The latest "religious feast" to have been celebrated in northern Nigeria, was reportedly ignited by the fanatical pronouncement of one Ahmed Sani, the Muslim governor of the north-eastern state of Zamfara, to the effect that his multiethnic and multi-religious enclave resort to "the Shariah," or Islamic law. Indeed, the problem with this sort of edict lies less in its ideological orientation—although the latter is admittedly significant—than its clash with an increasingly cosmopolitan and global cultural ethos. For instance, as the **New York Times** article noted, soon after Governor Sani's proclamation of Zamfara, one of 36 Nigerian states, "schools were segregated into single-sex institutions, hotels and bars stopped serving alcohol and taxis only for women began appearing on the streets of the state capital, Gusau. Last month [for instance], a man who was caught drinking alcohol in public received 80 lashes with a cane." Indeed, this kind of primitive jurisprudence very much characterized the 3-month Rawlings revolution of 1979, and again in 1981 and 1982, culminating only in the retrospectively redemptive assassination of the three Supreme Court justices and the quondam senior military officer.

The history of Islam and Christianity in northern Nigeria in particular, and continental Africa in general, is quite complex and thus can be neither amply delineated nor resolved in a cursory summative essay as this. I do not pretend to have discursively prepared myself for the historiographical intricacies that such a project requires, except to articulate my observations as a reasonably well-educated African of goodwill and the doting father of a daughter with a full-blooded Nigerian mother, whatever "full-blooded" means.

I first officially articulated my belief in the best remedy for many of Africa's so-called religious wars being the apriori acceptance of Africanity as extra-religious, with regard to either Christianity or Islam, in 1990. My views back then appeared in the magazine *African Profiles International*, a bona fide Nigerian monthly which continues to erroneously bill itself as an international African publication. For instance, when Mr. Kofi Annan, the veteran Ghanaian diplomat, was elected the first United Nations secretary-general from the so-called sub-Saharan or Black Africa, *Profiles* published a dolorously jaundiced editorial lamenting the fact that a better qualified Nigerian had not been selected. The fact that several years before Ghana had supported the appointment of a Nigerian, Chief Emeka Ayaoku, as secretary-general of the British Commonwealth of Nations did not seem to have mattered. Furthermore, the indelible historical fact that Ghana, not Nigeria, was the first "Black African" country to have joined the Commonwealth and the United Nations, also did not seem to mean much of anything to the Harvard-trained sociologist, editor-publisher of *African Profiles International*.

The tragic horror of the chronic Kaduna Riots, is also the collective tragedy of continental Africa's sociopolitical, economic and cultural destiny. In Nkrumahist parlance, until all Africans recognize this problem as such and literally pull the bull by the horns, global Africans are doomed to the fate of Sisyphus. In these circumstances, the hasty tendency on the part of many a prominent African scholar or political scientist has bee to assert military dictatorship as an immediate panacea. Our forty-plus years of experience with the execrable likes of Idi Amin, Gnassingbe Eyadema, Sani Abacha, Samuel Doe, Jerry Rawlings, Mobutu, Jammeh and Sankara, must make a little wiser. Indeed, in his otherwise erudite and comprehensive book and television documentary *The Africans: A Triple Heritage*, leading Kenyan political scientist Ali Mazrui noted that while military dictatorship in Nigeria, for instance, had tended to stifle productive national discourse and cultural creativity, the tenures of civic governments had often meant a dangerous and precipitous devolution from a welcome sense of order to outright social chaos and free-falling corruption.

The recent Nigerian conniption may be attributable to the fact that the grievances that precipitated the Biafran Civil War do not seem to have been resolved. Indeed, early this year (2000) Colonel Odumegwu Ojukwu, the man who led nearly one million (some have put the figure at about three millions) Ibos to their deaths between 1967 and 1970, told BBC World-Service Radio that he had never regretted his leadership role in this putatively extraneous massacre of the innocents. Rather, Colonel Ojukwu vaunted that as a 33-year-old Oxbridge-educated, angry Nigerian, he felt very justified to have pursued his ill-fated and bloody cause.

The Kaduna problem is also a problem of massive illiteracy. With the rate of formal schooling hovering in the dismal vicinity of 30-40-percent, and excruciatingly compounded by steady socioeconomic degeneration, as is the case in the entire region, that salutary culture of epistemological objectivity is woefully lacking. That Nigeria has been atomized or balkanized into 36 states—to better appreciate the enormity of this state of affairs, one needs to imagine a United States of America composed of 150 states—does not seem to have facilitated a well-needed geopolitical cohesion. The current trend and structure of African leadership, whereby career soldiers first shoot their way to power and then deck civic garbs to dance around the ballot box, even while still toting their bazookas and AK-47s does not augur well for the peace and prosperity of the continent. Mr. Olusegun Obasanjo, the current president of Nigeria, is an atavistic chip of the proverbial old block, in the pejorative sense of the term, though the former military strongman, during whose watch N 7Billion (Naira), more that $10billion in Nigerian currency vanished from the national treasury, is relatively more legitimate than almost any of his professional counterparts in the West African sub-region. Already, news reports bespeak of profuse formation of separatist political organizations. Does this sinister state of affairs portend another Biafra in the offing? One only hopes the senseless catastrophes of yesteryear have made us more mature and wiser. If not, the future must obviously seem quite troubling.

5

A New Meaning in Literacy

Socio-cultural decadence and moral atrophy seem to have dominated Ghanaian intellectual and journalistic circles for some time now. Oftentimes the tendency has been for self-styled "neo-patriots" to wistfully bemoan the current intellectual and cultural inadequacies. And if you are blunt like me, you may even be tempted to reduce this unfortunate phenomenon to the rather picturesque metaphor of "inferiority complex." It is almost as if we insist on claiming, quite chauvinistically, that we ought, perforce, to symbolize unparalleled African intellectual and cultural excellence. The trouble with this trend of reasoning is that it is woefully ahistorical, for it seems to suggest a brazen failure of the mature appreciation of the need to pay for our collective national misdemeanors and felonies over the years—at least for 34 sanguinary years now, and still counting.

Thus, I was hardly surprised not very long ago when I picked up an issue of the ***Ghanaian Chronicle*** and read the following portion of an article by one Kwesi Intsuah: "Not long ago, Ghanaians were the best educated in Black Africa; today Nigerians have far surpassed us in all areas of learning. That is one outcome of their bold temper. Look at the way they write—in journalism, in the novel and in dramatic forms—far, far better than anything you see in Ghana. On stage and in front of the camera, they act far better, with a nobler sense of humor, especially when it comes to laughing at themselves.

The article in question, titled "Rawlings and Abacha," dealt with what the writer presumed to be the no-nonsense, aggressive Nigerian national character which, to Intsuah, accounted for the high rate of Nigerian academic success in recent years. First of all, without quibbling about the veracity, relevance or validity of such semantically loaded geopolitical stereotyping, it may be of interest to ask: "Just how did this supposedly bold Nigerian national spirit bring about the high quality of literary works produced by the citizens of this 'great' West African country?"

In reality, Nigeria's current remarkable academic and socio-cultural successes parallel the Nkrumah-led development programs launched between the early 1950s and the mid-1960s. It included free universal elementary education up to the 10th grade for all able-bodied Ghanaians and other Africans and even non-Africans, including the then-hundreds of thousands of Nigerian immigrants as well as the battalions of Ghanaian-born Nigerians whom Professor K.A. Busia and his so-called Progress Party (PP) henchmen deported from our country in the early 1970s, under the PP's infamous Aliens' Compliance Order (ACO). Under this edict, non-Ghanaian West-African immigrants, largely Nigerians, who had entered the country when visas were superfluous, were given a year's deadline to regularize their stay or citizenship and residential status or find themselves pro-scribed and virtually rendered persona-non-grata. Visas had not been necessary during the colonial era when the Ghanaian capital of Accra served as the head-quarters of the so-called British West Africa—a geographically dispersed and inorganic agglomeration comprising of the Gambia, Sierra Leone, Nigeria and Ghana. These were also indisputably the richest geopolitical provinces in the West African sub-region, made up of some 16 countries. Britain administered these flesh-pot colonies as a federation, with the pound sterling the main cur-rency of commerce. Of course under British colonial governance, there was noth-ing like "citizenship" for the African person. At best, we were all considered "Crown Subjects," a rather more refined and sophisticated description of a serf or hostage. For, let no well-meaning person make any mistake, European colonial-ism was a shameless act of terrorism masquerading as Manifest Destiny, in the pseudo-religious, supremacist sense of the expression. Chinua Achebe, far and away the foremost Nigerian novelist, has often told the anecdotal story of having to travel during the late 1950s on foundation and study fellowship grants to countries like Australia, Britain and the United States, toting a passport which designated him "A British Subject." In sum, the immigration crisis set in motion by the Busia government, and which seems to have rapidly become a major retal-iatory fare of international discourse in West Africa, is purely an act of neo-colonial balkanization. Even our very identities as nationalities are minted of Western colonial expropriation; the African is, thus, pretty much an "Afropean," as a renowned African-American intellectual once put the matter.

Needless to say, since the retrospectively apocalyptic overthrow of Kwame Nkrumah's Convention People's Party (CPP) in 1966, Ghana has been on a dra-matic downward spiral at all levels of cultural endeavor, except perhaps in the seemingly pathological proliferation of Christian churches, as well as the latter's equally pathological pseudo-religious cottage, music industry. It is, however, significant to note that during the colonial period, the country's major Christian churches made remarkable contributions to our intellectual, professional and cultural development. Almost every distinguished Ghanaian statesman, technocrat or entrepreneur to have appeared on the public scene since the late 19th century until the immediate pre-and post-independence era was the veritable product of one Christian missionary institution or another. The problem with the post-independence era churches, however, is that only a few, if any, have been selflessly interested in initiating and pursuing such highly beneficial ventures as the massive establishment of schools and colleges. Often trucking by the generic designation of "revivalist" or "spiritual" churches, these establishments have shown themselves to be almost wholly interested in exploiting the poor and rudderless working class by preaching a fatalistic psychology of despair, in the name of some vaguely defined heavenly salvation. To be sure, this is very much a carry-over from the colonial era. However, the colonial churches had a leg up on these pseudo-modern, loudspeaker-blasting shamanistic clubs, in that the former made the material uplift of their congregants a vital block of their ideological agenda.

Furthermore, the country has witnessed the meteoric rise and fall of largely exploitative, neocolonialist regimes. There was the so-called National Liberation Council (NLC) junta, led by such political and intellectual midgets as A. A. Afrifa, Ankrah, Acheampong and E. K. Kotoka, whose pre-eminent defense of Nkrumah's overthrow was that the Osagyefo had threatened to herd Ghana out of the neocolonialist British Commonwealth of Nations (see Chinweizu's *The West and the Rest of Us*). Consequently, the NLC spent three apocalyptic years in power almost indiscriminately dismantling every major seminal project initiated by the CPP government, using public or the proverbial tax-payer's money. Among the dismantled projects was the Ghana Atomic Energy Plant at Kwabenya, near the nation's capital of Accra, a program which aimed at developing medical, agricultural and technological research. The NLC also abandoned the hundreds of Russian-made fishing trawlers purchased with tax-payers' money for the development of the Ghana Fishing Corporation. And although the coup was alleged to have been sponsored by the United States government, via its Central Intelligence Agency (CIA), no Marshall Plan, like the one Washington emplaced for the massive and rapid reconstruction of a shell-battered post-World War II Europe and Japan, was accorded Ghana's massively damaged economy and infrastructure. Later on, the Busia-led Progress Party regime would methodically supervise the wastage of almost every constructive project that Nkrumah initiated (see Ebo Hutchful's *Ghana And The IMF*). It is also significant to observe that after the July 17, 1956 general elections that positioned Nkrumah's Convention

People's Party as the first post-independence government, the Oxbridge-educated Dr. K. A. Busia led a delegation, largely instigated by the reactionary leadership of Dr. J. B. Danquah's United Gold Coast Convention (UGCC), to London's Colonial Office, to petition the British government not to grant independence to Ghana (see *Forward Ever: The Life of Kwame Nkrumah.* London: Panaf Books, 1977). Professor Busia, a self-proclaimed staunch adherent of parliamentary democracy, would also weigh in on the side of the NLC government which toppled the CPP as an organizing consultant on civic education and leadership. He would also be accused of being the first, and perhaps only, Ghanaian premier on record to have drawn an entire year's salary in bulk before any commensurate work had been performed.

Nigeria, on the other hand, has been steadily engaged in constructive public programs since the 1960s, beginning with the U.S.-funded University of Nigeria at Nsukka (see Chinweizu's *The West and the Rest of Us*). Even in the heat of the country's catastrophic civil war, in which an excess of one million people—some scholars put the figure at five million—lost their lives, massive development projects were still very much the norm. And by the late 1970s and 1980s when Ghana's ramshackle economy could no longer sustain any viable and qualitative educational system, Nigeria was awash in oil and had just embarked on a free-education program from elementary to tertiary levels, almost a xerographic copy of Nkrumah's much-maligned programs of the 1950s and '60s. Thus Nigeria's current socioeconomic and cultural successes may be more attributable to sound governmental policies initiated by that country's leadership, both civilian and military, than being just the direct result of any "bold temper," as Kwesi Intsuah would have his Ghanaian audience believe.

If by "bold temper" Mr. Intsuah implies a well-focused collective national will to success, then the writer might be quite apt in his assessment. For during the past two decades that Mr. Rawlings' so-called National Democratic Congress (NDC), and before that the nominally ironic Provisional National Defense Council (PNDC), has been in power, tertiary or college-level education has virtually ground to a halt, even as the government also continued to tinker recklessly with elementary education. Relatively, Nigeria has fared far better; for during the same period in question, that country more than doubled physical facilities at the tertiary educational level. Whether the quality of pedagogy has been evenly spread or distributed remains moot. The massive influx of Ghanaian educators and academics into Nigeria, and the converse impoverishment of its Ghanaian coordinate by efflux, the proverbial brain-drain, can obviously not be gainsaid. Indeed, I, for one, hardly know any Nigerian who has been resident in the

United States over the past two decades who did not at least have one Ghanaian teacher in college or high school.

The preceding notwithstanding, ever since I can remember, Nigerians have always bested Ghanaians in the field of literary production. Even the seminal English grammar textbooks used in Ghanaian elementary and secondary schools were written by authors with Yoruba-Nigerian names like Ogundipe. Of course, in fields like history and the other humanities, Ghanaian-authored textbooks have been quite predominant. The fact that Nigeria's population has been pegged at seven times that of Ghana's, has often been invoked as an excuse for the recently dismal performance of the latter. However, it is interesting to also observe that some thirty-five to forty years ago when Ghana's populational ratio to Nigeria's was even much smaller, the former bested the latter in most of the standardized examinations administered by the West African Examinations Council (WAEC). Ghana also routinely trounced Nigeria at soccer meets, both informally and officially, well into the 1970s. Indeed, the only period during which Ghanaian literary output outpaced Nigeria's was prior to the 1950s, which period witnessed the phenomenal rise of such remarkable writers and thinkers as J. E. Casely-Hayford, R. E. G. Armattoe, Gladys Casely-Hayford, J. C. deGraft, Efua Theodora Sutherland, and Michael Dei-Anang, among a host of others. If contemporary Ghanaian writers do not comfortably rival their Ghanaian counterparts, there may be several plausible reasons for this.

First of all, with a population six to seven times the size of Ghana's, as aforementioned, Nigeria has a larger pool of talent and a viable reader's market to feed the former. Secondly, and perhaps even more significantly, most distinguished Nigerian writers, such as Soyinka, Achebe, Okri, Ogundipe Leslie-Molara, Sulu Sofola, and Niyi Osundare have either spent extensive periods abroad studying and honing their artistry, and thus becoming widely exposed to Western, classical literary forms, or worked with such multi-national publishers as Longmans, MacMillan, and Oxford University Press. It is important to observe that all the preceding publishers, and a number of others herein unlisted, have overseas offices and branches in Nigeria and a few other African countries, but not in Ghana. Prominent among the category of West African writers who have worked intimately with Western publishing houses are Achebe, Okigbo and Okpewho. Most Ghanaian writers have had no such salutary opportunities. This may also be largely due to Nkrumah's ideological socialism which alienated many multinational publishers, as well as Ghana's relatively small commercial book market which is not very attractive to large publishers. But perhaps more importantly, unlike Ghana, Nigeria has had an extensive and long-established indigenous book-publishing industry, otherwise known as the Onitsha Market Literature.

Finally, regarding the relatively poor development of journalism in Ghana vis-à-vis Nigeria, the problem may seem to be unmistakably political. Traditionally, as attested by Wole Soyinka and others, Nigerian governments have been more tolerant of the media than their Ghanaian counterparts, though in both countries there have been memorable, if also traumatic, cases of brutal media clampdown. The shameful and tragic cases of Dele Giwa and John Kugblenu readily come to mind. It is, however, envisaged that the current proliferation of print and electronic media, particularly within the private sector, is likely to rectify such perceived imbalances. Two years ago when this writer visited Ghana, that nation's capital of Accra alone boasted of some eight (8) FM-radio stations; except for the so-called GAR-radio, owned by the government, all the stations were known to be wholly owned and operated by private entrepreneurs and companies. Of course, as was to be expected, word from the grapevine indicated that some stations, particularly those purportedly owned by resident non-Ghanaians, were actually bona fide fronts for either cabinet members of government or other top political functionaries. Indeed, this writer was privileged to be featured on at least five of these stations, including one run by the nation's flagship academy, the University of Ghana, and was quite happy to report to his friends and colleagues that these stations, largely run by young people between the ages of 18 and 45, were delightfully giving their governmental counterparts the proverbial run for their money.

The fact that in Ghana, unlike Nigeria, until very recently journalism was considered to be the preserve of the "intellectual underclass," mainly people with weak or marginal high school diplomas, and therefore people who had miserably failed to gain admission into one of the three major national universities, signified that the inky profession in Ghana would be neither highly energetic and creative nor even simply exciting. Over and above all, however, if the demonstrably myopic NDC government desists from its constant and riotous closures of Ghanaian universities upon the least perceived act of provocation as well as its rampant harassment and arbitrary imprisonment of journalists, often on trumped-up charges, it is hoped that our intellectual, esthetic and cultural development would, once again, become both the envy and model for the rest of Africa.

6

Every Misfortune Is A Revelation

In June 2000, a Ghanaian Fokker-27, a military aircraft, to be certain, was reported to have crash-landed at the Accra International Airport in that country's capital. To-date, the Accra airport, constructed during the much-maligned Nkrumah administration, remains the only airstrip with "international" status, to be sure, marginally so. As adumbrated in the preceding essays, Kwame Nkrumah is the phenomenological or historical coordinate of the proverbial Nile river, which is inextricably identified with the geo-economic and political survival of Egyptians and, indeed, the entire eastern region of the African continent. Mr. Rawlings, who will be standing down come the end of the 2000 general elections, will almost certainly go down the annals of Ghanaian politics as the most astute, if also murderously mercurial, ideological chameleon. The late prominent attorney Joseph Appiah, affectionately known to most Ghanaians as Joe Appiah, used to "own" that accolade. The latter was called a "political chameleon" because he did not seem to be highly principled in the context of Ghanaian politics. Indeed, Chameleon Joe was known to have served in every government, military or civilian since the country's independence in 1957 until the late 1970s, when he served in some protean sort of capacity as a member of the Council-of-State, a rudimentary Ghanaian coordinate of the British House of Lords, from whence this veritable house-of-cards acquired its inspiration. The Ghanaian breed, unlike its British counterpart which is composed of the aristocracy, is largely made up of superannuated political functionaries who, by the stroke of either collective, pathological amnesia of the national mnemonic psyche, or lackeys and flunkies who require some sense of social self-worth, often after having been virtually written off the leadership landscape. They are almost akin to the so-called veterans of the liberation struggle in such southern African countries as Zimbabwe, South Africa and Mozambique. They undeniably played critical roles in their countries' harrowing stride towards African self-rule; however, because of decades of socio-cultural mal-nourishment or the lack of adequate preparation for modern leader-ship, for they also tend to possess the most rudimentary intellectual orientation, these elements often do not qualify to hold any cabinet, judicial and diplomatic positions. Ironically, it is these very elements who catapulted the liberation strug-gle to its logical conclusion, who also became the literal enemies of the state. They, undeniably deserve substantial compensation from their government; simultaneously, however, like enslaved diasporic Africans nearly two centuries before, these veterans seem to have effectively outlived their usefulness. Their ideological and practical relevance ended with the success of the revolution. And since over the course of time, as the revolution transcends national boundaries and meets with the practical realities of international politics, a new crop of lead-ership perforce emerges—a leadership corps of highly-trained lawyers, teachers, physicians and bureaucrats—it—stands to reason that the veteran becomes the veritable figment of yesteryear's freedom dream. The devious machinations of the erstwhile colonialist ensure that, short of taking the law into their own hands, as it were, the irritable veteran never crosses over into the modern, post-colonial world. If we cannot perpetuate our Manifest Destiny of African enslavement, the situation seems to imply, then those who are responsible for the premature demise of European supremacy ought not to relish their sacrilege.

All this is another way of saying that the Ghanaian military plane that crash-landed at the Accra International Airport, killing six of its 52 passengers (*Afri-can-American Observer* June 6-12, 2000: 13), was a tragedy that told a story beyond its raw wreckage. For starters, the Fokker-27 aircraft was being used for commercial purposes, a quite bizarre form of military capitalism, particularly when one takes into account the fact that Mr. Rawlings's pseudo-civic adminis-tration is in reality a constitutional stratocracy, for the Ghanaian president merely converted his so-called Provisional National Defense Council (PNDC) and the latter's National Commission for Democracy into the all too logical National Democratic Congress (NDC). To be sure, there is absolutely nothing wrong with converting a Ghanaian military aircraft into a domestic commercial airliner, the Ghanaian soldier in the post-Nkrumah era is merely a white elephant, a petty thug and terrorist against unarmed market women and the general civilian popu-lace. Which means that the Fokker-27 which crash-landed was not worth its insignia or legend. Indeed, the primal attempt at using the Ghanaian armed forces for military intervention ended in woeful failure in Liberia in the early 1980s. To-date, the army's participation in Sierra Leone and other troubled spots on both the continent and abroad has been largely rump-like or supportive.

Thus, in using the plane for lucrative commercial purposes, the top-echelons of that establishment had drawn the sagacious conclusion regarding the fact that the Ghana army, as it now operates, is otiose to the national political culture. Indeed, the post-Nkrumah Ghanaian military is composed largely of persons with little or no intellectual depth vis-à-vis the country's collective national responsibility—the institution's leadership by and large lacks a critical sense of the global dynamics of political economy, and since they have been trained to sophomorically believe that: "A soldier walks on his stomach," any extra-gastro-intestinal phenomenon becomes terra incognito. In fact, the preceding sentiment undergirds almost all military interventions in Africa and most of the so-called Third World.

The foregoing notwithstanding, and perhaps even at the risk of sounding "nationalistic" in the mildly pejorative sense of the term, one cannot downplay the proverbial "manifest destiny" of Ghanaian political leadership in the West African sub-region, a coveted niche largely negotiated by founding premier Kwame Nkrumah. The apparent dramatic recession of the country from active international political participation has also witnessed the dramatic and, some well-meaning Ghanaians might also acknowledge, traumatic marginalization of the country and its people. Interestingly, the fate and destiny of modern Ghana are inextricably woven into the general historiographical fabric of the continent. President Nkrumah unmistakably ensured this on the eve of Ghana's independence on March 5, 1957, when the firebrand pan-Africanist asserted that: "The independence of Ghana [was] meaningless unless it [was] linked up with the total liberation of the African continent." And this is also why this writer finds it utterly difficult to stanch his unremitting contempt for those of his countryfolk who would have the rest of their compatriots and the world, at large, believe that Ghana's recent plight is the result of some supposedly overweening ambition of President Nkrumah to dominate continental African politics, instead of assuming the rather callow and parochial, if also sophomoric, mantle of micro-nationalism. To be certain, it is the woeful inability of the Ghanaian opposition leadership to transcend the solipsistic politics of tribalism that has facilitated—partially—the Rawlings dictatorship over the past twenty years. And it is painful to admit, but the pseudo-democratic government of the so-called National Democratic Congress is likely to prevail for a while, at least until two significant changes occur on the national political landscape. One, the definitive and temporal removal, a purely providential act, of the current egocentric and pathologically myopic leadership, bi-partisanly, from the national political stage. And two, the salutary emergence of a younger corps of politicians, particularly among the membership of the opposition, who have a broader and global perspective on both Ghanaian and African political culture.

In the final analysis, the Ghanaian military aircraft that went down in June 2000, might have gone down with part of the lurid history of greed which has characterized that institution for the past forty years. On the other hand and, perhaps even more significantly, what Ghanaians demand to know is precisely whose business it was to manage the finances of that ill-fated Fokker (no pun intended) 27. For it was not clear from news-reports whether the latter was integrally operated or controlled by Ghana Airways Corporation.

7

A Question of Language

Arrogantly speaking, I have been writing some of the best contemporary poetry ever written in English, which no one seems to care to buy or even distribute. Not long ago, a novelist-bookseller who decided to become a novelist because the American book market did not seem to be interested in his artistry, directed me to two African-American book distributors whom Mr. Joe Fortune-Hunter believed might be interested in facilitating my access to the market. For several weeks after these distributors had asked me to ship samples of my books for their examination and decision, I hadn't heard from either one of them. So one day I mustered a tad of courage to follow up on my compliance and learn what they each had in store for me. Needless to say, I had my own misgivings shipping my books to these distributors. And, to be certain, the kindly Mr. Joe Fortune-Hunter had not hesitated to let me understand from the get-go that taking his advice by communicating with the two Black distributors who, by the way, were his major dealers, might not be such a fruitful idea, after all. "First of all," said Fortune-Hunter, "The poetry market is not robust. I used to write poetry myself. No publisher would take it, so I began writing novels, and so far the going has been great!"

Joe Fortune-Hunter encouraged me to try my hands at some kind of fiction, particularly the formulaic but commercially hot sort of fiction penned by the likes of Jerome Eric Dickey. You know what I mean? The type of lachrymose fiction in which rogue men and unsuspecting, love-famished "sisters" run around in circles looking for romance and love but end up harvesting raw sex and utter disappointment. This often happens because both authors and characters are invariably vague regarding the meaning of "love" and "romance." Not infrequently, both terms designate a seemingly endless pleasure binge. The idea of growth and maturity seems to underscore the themes of such novels, such as Mr. Dickey's **The Cheaters**, though one is not quite sure whether such an honorable theme is invariably accorded short-shrift in view of the callow demands of the yellow-literature market. The idiom of such novels is campy and quite realistic, though this element of verisimilitude seems to be pursued more for the simple reason of duplication rather than moral or emotional transcendence, the kind of Shakespearean catharsis that one garners from most good and all great literature.

But the preceding is not even the focus of this essay, except on the question of language and ideology and their indubitable implications for our waning civilization—what Harvard University scholar Cornel West terms "this culture of instant gratification." Recently, an article appeared in **The New York Times** (July 18, 2000) titled "Clash of Styles in a Coming Presidential Race." It was about a raging political contest between President Yoweri Museveni, of Uganda, a long-time guerrilla war leader and for a half-generation the de facto strongman of that resourceful but war-torn country of the Great Lakes region. Mainstream America seems to harbor the kind of fatuous admiration for President Museveni that one often has for a speaking parakeet, or even a monkey who shows a deft appreciation for a human gimmick or two. And Africa, in the psyche of the average mainstream American, is a kind of wild botanical garden and zoo combined. In recent years, it has become quite fashionable to hop onto a New York City subway and find glossy photographs advertising the scenic beauty of "Congolese Africans." Make no mistake, the Africans in these pictures look nowhere near you and I, the human species, that is. They are phalanges of chimpanzees and baboons imported into the United States and stocked in the artificial jungles of the Bronx, in a primitivized pocket called The Congo. There is no adjectival prefix of "Democratic" or "Republic" affixed to Bronx's Congo. For an African traditionalist with a high sense of self-worth and dignity, the Bronx's Congo is nothing short of an unpardonable insult, its advertising, or commercial, import notwithstanding. One does not visit anywhere in the world and see a bunch of pathological cannibals or necrophiliacs indiscriminately shooting at each other in pictures designated: "The United States of America."

America's apparent "love" for President Museveni seems to be predicated on the fact that the Ugandan chieftain spent years in the forest fighting the infamous government of President Idi Amin, the man Americans and some Asians, particularly Indians and Pakistanis, love to hate. The fact that Mr. Museveni's government is an objective replica of Gen. Amin's means less to America than the fact that the former seems to have opened up his country for inordinate foreign exploitation, with the United States being one of the major beneficiaries. In this sense, President Museveni could be aptly represented as the quintessential neocolonialist, the sort of African leader who represents the interests of foreign governments and investors. Indeed, the great Central African Region seems to have produced an unprecedented number of neocolonialist leaders—i.e. Bokassa, Tshombe and Mobutu. A little eastwards, in Kenya, even one such leader had the temerity to publicly conflagrate tons of foreign exchange-fetching ivory tusks a while ago, simply to fatuously prove to the West that Africans were morally sound when it comes to preserving the corporeal integrity of our wildlife. We have yet to be told whether any of the wealthy Western instigators of such economic treason has offered to pay for Mr. Arap Moi's politics of geekdom.

In Uganda, like many of his compatriots, Mr. Nasser Ntege Sebaggala, a former mayor of Kampala, is seeking to oust President Museveni, who has been running the country since 1986. For ***The New York Times*** the fact that Mr. Museveni is a graduate of Tanzania's University of Dar es Salem is more important than the fact that Museveni belongs to that crop of highly educated, actually literate, self-serving posse of neocolonialist dictators who have virtually stalled socio-economic and cultural development on the continent over the past two generations. Consequently, in comparing the two major political players in the Ugandan ideological theater, ***New York Times***' Ian Fisher wrote: "Mr. Museveni, in office since he fought his way to power in 1986, graduated from Dar es Salem University in Tanzania and is able to make campaign speeches into little history lessons. His English is flawless. He is a military man, while Mr. Sebaggala is a businessman. Mr. Museveni's career was in many ways formed against the dictatorship of Idi Amin in the 1970s, while Mr. Sebaggala's businesses did quite well then."

In the preceding, the obvious implication is that somehow Mr. Sebaggala's sentiments belong to the infamous and quite socio-politically hermetic era of the Amin regime. The fact that Mr. Sebaggala supposedly prospered under a nationalistic atmosphere that stanched the economic excesses of the West implicitly renders the latter guilty of communism. In this sense Mr. Sebaggala the ideologue, and this writer does not pretend to be privy to such knowledge, is no different from such illustrious predecessors as Nkrumah, Nasser, Toure, Kenyatta, Lumumba, Neto and Cabral, among others. Which is not to put Mr. Sebaggala in the august and revered league of the foregoing political patriarchs.

That Mr. Museveni graduated from Dar es Salem University is almost no big deal; the East African Harvard of Makerere is right inside Uganda and has been there long for nearly four generations. Indeed it was the latter university that produced leading African political theorist Ali A. Mazrui, of Kenya. So, for many Ugandans the idea of a flawless African education is not in Tanzania. Makerere also produced such leading East African literary giants as Ngugi wa Thiong'O, of Kenya, and Okot p'Bitek, of Uganda.

Then also, Mr. Fisher of *The New York Times* describes Mr. Sebaggala as "a convicted fraud" who is "not well educated" [sic]. It is interesting to appreciate the fact that for the *New York Times* and many other Americans, a well-educated person is one who speaks "flawless English," even if such idiomatic felicity is bereft of content, just like the idiomatically flawless Scottish-descended former dictator of a very important West African country who is well-liked by many African-Americans because, as one friend tragically told this writer a while back, "The guy has no accent," which simply means that President Harold Churchill speaks with a Western accent, in of itself a striking mark of cultural civility.

Actually, unlike what Mr. Ian Fisher, of *The New York Times,* would have the world believe, Mr. Nasser Ntege Sebaggala is not "a convicted fraud," unless, of course, one also believes that before Nelson Mandela, Robert Mugabe, Agostinho Neto, and Sam Nujoma, for instance, assumed premiership of their respective countries, these post-colonial African leaders were the "terrorists" that Washington and London wanted the rest of the world to know and mark down with red-ink.

Indeed, in 1998 while attending an international conference on garbage disposal in his capacity as mayor of Kampala, Uganda's largest metropolis, Mr. Sebaggala was arrested in Boston and "charged with passing eight fraudulent checks worth $44,000" and made to serve a year in an American stir. It is quite reasonable to surmise that had Mr. Sebaggala been the chief of a major European, Arabic or Asian metropolis, the outcome of his trial would have been quite different. More so, when one recognizes the fact that, as reported by *New York Times'* Ian Fisher, the sum of $44,000 dud traveler's checks, for which Mayor Sebaggala served a year's prison term, was part of a humongous $2.5million worth of genuine checks he then issued. And when we backtrack to April 1998 and learn that Mr. Sebaggala had trounced Christopher Iga, President Museveni's favorite candidate in the mayoral elections, Mr. Sebaggala's conviction and sentencing fall squarely in place. It may not necessarily have been a conspiracy to destroy or tarnish the popular image of a man whose "businesses did quite well" under the Amin regime, but one cannot also easily accept the judicial railroading of Mr. Sebaggala as a complete act of nature. Of course, we also know that "nature" works in mysterious ways. Thus, when Ian Fisher observes that: "The truth is, he is popular because of his flaws, not to mention a well-honed populist touch. [And that] In the same way that some Americans may see a bit of themselves in Bill Clinton's indiscretions, some Ugandans who feel left behind in the nation's slow economic revival embrace the entire package of Mr. Sebaggala. [That] They actually like the idea that he may have stolen $44,000 in one of the world's richest countries, we know that the visceral idea of a veritable and viable existence of a critical African moral imagination lies squarely beyond the pale of the average mainstream American perspective. Purportedly "stealing" the puny sum of $44,000 from the world's greatest theft-prone country, and here the allusion is to the historical enslavement of Africans, is obviously far less significant than the Afrocentric imperative for Africans to determine their own collective scale of values. Thus in African politics, the superficial question of idiomatic eloquence in alien tongues is far less important than veritable linguistic content cast within the existential context of pragmatic leadership. This is the indubitable objective of global Africans on the threshold of the twenty-first century.

8

The Trouble With Ghana

Two years ago (1998), when I started serializing my perspectives and reflections on Ghanaian politics and culture, a number of my countrymen and women who had been following my submissions accosted me, publicly and privately, with the earnest request that I explain to them just what were the basic problems plaguing our beloved country. More importantly, these people often appeared quizzical in their search for an appreciable knowledge regarding the specific nature of the remedies needed to put their country on a sound socio-economic, political and cultural footing. Unfortunately, invariably when they have approached me, many of these self-professing patriots have seemed to be so set in their ideological proclivities that what they have ended up doing is to simply assert their "religious" affiliation or moral identification with either one of the two major Ghanaian political parties—the ruling National Democratic Congress (NDC) and the New Patriotic Party (NPP). One such interlocutor even suggested to me, with the intransigent fervor of a grizzled party hack, that the sole reason for President Rawlings' "maladministrative" longevity was due to some curious lack of any viable leadership alternative among the entire talent pool of Ghanaian citizenry. It was almost as if the honorable, albeit grossly misguided, gentleman was implying that so godsend was Mr. Rawlings that without the latter's fabled existence, there would be no such polity going by the historic designation of "Ghana."

Several years ago, a renowned City University of New York professor of African Studies, who also happens to be a benevolent and avuncular friend of mine, suggested to me, almost alarmingly, that it would be meed if I held off any criticism of Mr. Rawlings and his NDC henchmen and women, because without the latter's gracious governance, Ghana could easily devolve into another Rwanda or Somalia. I had to remind my dear friend that if anything at all, it was the perennial entrenchment of such stratocracies as the NDC, rather than their absence or dearth, that bode ill for the country's administrative future. Needless to say, my senior academic colleague, friend and former mentor, had befriended a traditional Ghanaian chieftain who also happened to be a cabinet member of the ruling government. Actually, the aforementioned chieftain, who also happens to be a good friend of my companion, could be more aptly described as a pseudo-traditional Ghanaian chieftain. Not only is he Western-schooled, but more disturbingly, our traditional cultural custodian shows every daunting sign of the miseducated. Almost never a year passes by without encountering this gentleman at a riotous social function, either here in the proverbial Big Apple, or elsewhere among other bland and blasé Ghanaian expatriates, if there were any such phenomena, which I guess there must be. In short, the man is your vintage party animal.

So staunch and intimate is their friendship that not very long ago, my professorial friend, a diasporic African, as he prefers to be called among the continental African public, was enstooled as **Nkosohene** (or Doyen of progress, the rough-coordinate of a secretary for works and housing in mainstream American political idiom) in the Ghanaian district of the NDC stalwart chieftain. The latter is even rumored to have constructed an Olympic-size swimming pool for a phalanx of diasporic Africans, all of whom have been named chiefs in his mini-republic. The reason? The tropical Ghanaian climate is too sultry for these royals, most of whom were, by the way, born in Georgia, Louisiana and Alabama! It is almost as if our "modern" chieftain has never experienced eastern-seaboard summer here in the United States. Of course, the whole drift of the preceding is to simply answer the rather bromidic question: "What is the trouble with Ghana?"

The first tack or approach is purely political, if one may say so, that is, one of responsive and responsible leadership. It goes almost without saying that one tragic index of intellectual and cultural under-development is when every Jato, Arkaah or Kufuor past the nominal age of puberty insists on forming a political party, in order to be elected life-president of Ghana. And, believe me, these people have been literally working off their behinds, all their lives, just to sit in the praetor's chair in the Big House which used to be the exit-point of our star-crossed diasporic ancestors during the days of slavery.

Needless to say, it was soldiers like Mr. Rawlings who taught the rest of us this soft-brained approach to leadership by mustering a few bandits, shooting their godforsaken way into the Castle (or the Ghanaian equivalent of the White House), and reducing every other Ghanaian into an abject state of perennial panic. During the much-maligned 1992 presidential election, for instance, nearly 15 political parties (they looked more than ragtag gangster groups) contested against Mr. Rawlings and his (P)NDC. Interestingly, almost every one of these opposition parties had the single pathetic agenda of wresting raw power from the bullish grips of the incumbent. Not surprisingly, they all flunked miserably, not because their common arch-nemesis had done anything substantive for the Ghanaian people, but simply because they had woefully forgotten the unimpeachable truth that Ghanaian politics, these days, subsists purely on relentless, browbeating demagoguery. But, make no mistake, Mr. Rawlings would not have hesitated declaring a state of emergency and inundating the principal localities with his praetorian posse, otherwise known as the Makola-raping Ghana Armed Forces.

Thus, while Mr. Rawlings went on the hustings promising unctuously to convert piped water into Baskin-Robbins' ice-cream sundaes, and every polytechnic institute and teacher-training college into full-fledged doctorate-awarding institutions, many an opposition presidential candidate was fired up with such personal vitriol as impeached the filial or natal legitimacy of Mr. Rawlings. Indeed, the NPP leader was even reported to have accused Mr. Rawlings of being "the son of a harlot," almost as if the target of abuse had preordained his own "unfortunate" parentage. And, of course, it goes without saying that this benighted kind of foul-mouthing hardly exudes presidential caliber. And to be frank, I was quite amused to see Mr. Rawlings mercilessly trounce his Oxbridge-educated archrival.

There are, of course, more than a phalanx of alternatives to the rather vision-less rulership of President Jerry John Rawlings. In 1992, for instance, it was the gratuitous NPP candidacy of Professor A. Adu-Boahen, arguably Ghana's foremost historian, that enabled Mr. Rawlings to easily negotiate his extra-judicial dictatorship into acrobatic constitutional legitimacy, at least on the face of things. That a University of London Ph.D. like Adu-Boahen could fathom a fair presidential run against a formidable military dictator, who had been misruling the country for nearly 11 years without the grace of a democratically sanctioned constitution, more than boggles the minds of well-meaning observers and citizens. In fact, such reckless, if also glaringly fatuous, intellectual temperament or orientation may have something to do with the NDC government's abject neglect of Ghanaian institutions of higher learning. For if our universities and colleges are wont to producing intellectual enigmas like Adu-Boahen, then who could intelligently argue against the calculatedly stubborn refusal of the NDC government to commit adequate resources to facilitate the long overdue modernization of our flagship academies?

What is even more aggravating is that people like Kufuor and the late Dr. Hilla Limann, who began "serving" their country in executive capacities during their late 20s and early 30s, refused to appreciate the simple fact that the end of their active political tenure was long overdue. Of course, one may legitimately argue that these "damaged goods" have a right, just like every other Ghanaian, to run for presidential office, however old or hulkingly grizzled they may be. Fair enough! But could the same case be made for a man who makes capital nonsense of constitutional democracy by shooting his way to power, and then 11 years later calls for the drafting of a new constitution to legitimize his own military dictatorship? Indeed, our greatest problem may be that cynical, so-called Consultative Assembly that drafted the current Constitution of the so-called Fourth Republic and reduced the traditional pedigree and other citizenship requirements to rubbles, in order to enable Mr. Rawlings to entrench his de facto dictatorship, thereby hijacking and stultifying our collective national destiny.

The West, of course, has not played a meliorating role in the continent's current dilemma, though the crux was indisputably concocted by the former's capitalist imperialism. Recently, an American "expert" on African affairs, for example, declared Angola and Nigeria to be "sub-Saharan" Africa's most strategic interest to the United States. By this, of course, was meant that these two countries were prime grist for economic exploitation, otherwise known as investment. Nigeria is said to have received, by African standards in these matters, from Western perspective, that is, a whopping $200million in development aid from Washington since Mr. Olusegun Obasanjo became the first elected president in twenty years, last year (**New York Times: Week in Review** 8/27/00). We are not told what form or shape the preceding aid assumed. Nothing, by way of American aid, is linked in the said report, written by Blaine Harden, to Angola; and one can reasonably surmise that this might be because Angola is in the proverbial eye of the storm. But what is significant, regarding the meaning of "interest" in American ideological idiom, is the fact that currently, "oil from Nigeria and Angola accounts for about 16 percent of America's supply." And that is a lot knowing the suicidal extremes to which George Bush, Sr., was willing to take the U.S. military during the early 1990s, when Iraqi president Saddam Hussein threatened to arrest American motor neurons, as it were. Hundreds of thousands of Iraqis, both civilian and military, are reported to have been buried alive in the desert, while American soldiers only returned with a glancing but rather irritating bugbear called "The Gulf-War Syndrome." It is alarming to further learn that oil supply from Nigeria and Angola is likely to shortly rise to a "projected figure" of more than 25 percent. Will America then be willing to do the peacekeeping beat if a Biafran-type carnival erupted in Nigeria, in particular, and the West African subregion in general? Of course, your guess is as good as mine.

Whatever the preceding scenario may mean in Africa's future development, there is something quite sinister about it. For five-hundred years, Africa was far and away America's top priority, as far as national interests went. That is, until the mid-nineteenth century when our cargo-humanity was suddenly rendered superfluous by industrial machinery. Thus, for Africans, to be at the top on the list of countries worthy of America's interest cannot be a very good thing. Unless, of course, one is fortunate enough to be designated "an ally" by Washington, which is just another way of saying "partner." Then again, what use could a patrician in partnership with a pauper have for the latter? Which is why it is not surprising to learn that: "The Republican majority in Congress has repeatedly cut [President Clinton's] budget requests for Africa and has so far failed to approve an administrative proposal to forgive about $475million in African debt" (*Week in Review* 8/27/00). Of course, such academic gesture could bring a false sense of relief to the grossly famished African soul. Then what happens on the dinner-table come sunset?

Indeed, it is quite tempting to blame "papal" Republicans like Jesse Helms, John Kasich, and good, old Strom Thurmond for the blistering blight on the African economic landscape. I, for one, didn't like it a bit when Mr. Helms put his arm on the shoulders of U. N. Secretary-General Kofi Annan and promised that Congress would make good on its dues default to that august world organization. America does not seem to be a respecter of global comity or decency. I only read this from the fact that four years later, Mr. Helms' Congress has yet to make good on America's leadership commitment to the United Nations Organization, the very brainchild of a legendary American president, I suppose.

But the problem is neither a Republican nor a Democratic one; it is simply a human problem—the problem of those who have often wanted more, even if having more could kill or maim. America is drowning in wealth, and pelf, even as the rest of the non-Western world goes to bed every night with growling stomachs. The problem is neither a Republican or Democratic problem. President Kennedy gave Africa the Peace Corps; and then he turned around shortly thereafter and destroyed whatever good the Peace Corps brought by sicking the CIA on our best and brightest...Nkrumah, Lumumba.... The problem is neither a Republican nor Democratic problem—my people, the problem is simply Human, and we are, indeed, all too Human! And so, now, who is really the problem?

9

Familial Dirt

There is that ageless proverb which exhorts that: "One does not wash one's dirty linen in public." Of course, not every race or culture holds the linen in the highest regard; which means that for some of us, we would rather wash our dirty linen in public than our **Kente** stole or cloth. The **Kente** is the royal fabric among the Akan-speaking people of Ghana. It is woven of silk. Tradition has it that the very first among our people to weave the **Kente** learned it by observing the spider weave its web. Which is quite an interesting story, because among the Akan the spider, or Ananse, is not quite your enterprising or diligent role-model. Ananse, in Akan folklore and philosophy, embodies all that is characteristic of the misanthrope and crassly antisocial—i.e. inordinate greed and avarice, unwillingness to share or compromise, and the primitive will to dominate at all costs. For these reasons, sometimes I even imagine Ananse to be the patriarch of some of our globally notorious, fanatical religious leaders who would have everything their own way or the highway, as it were.

The pejorative image of Ananse in Akan folk-philosophy is primarily instructive or propaedeutic; Ananse is that iconic template that instructs individuals in a societal setting what not to do in order to foster communal cooperation and ultimate prosperity, socially, spiritually and economically. The idea of *identity* is one that is of utmost importance to the Akan; and to the Akan the concept of identity is collective: one's social worth is more dependent on the checkered fortunes of one's ethnic group across the generations. On a smaller is the **Clan**, an association of people who lay claim to a common mythological ancestor. Often, among the Akan, who are ideologically matriarchal, that common ancestor is actually an *ancestress*, a woman. They [i.e. ancestors] also tend to be faceless and nameless, perhaps the result of oral traditional, mnemonic transience. Things and events written down, in whatever form, invariably have a way of outlasting memory, diachronic distortions notwithstanding. The **Clan** is so loosely organized and, in reality, so diffuse and cross-cultural as to almost pale in substance or significance vis-à-vis the ethnic group. And yet, paradoxically, without owning membership in a recognizable clan, one can almost stake no valid claim to one's Akan ethnicity. It is almost like claiming to be British without being able to point towards one's ancestral hearth or village. Of course in the modern era, when citizenship is merely an act of passport ownership, such "rootless" or moorless claim could be intelligently negotiated.

It, therefore, appears that in the final analysis, among the Akan the most important civic institutions are the ethnic group and the "sub-extended family." The latter terminology is rendered necessary because the Akan designation for "Family," called *Abusua,* connotes more than father, mother and siblings. For in Akan cultural idiom, the nuclear family does not exist as such; the most accurate descriptive for a family comprised of father, mother and siblings, is the "Household," or "Homestead." For the nuclear family is merely a branch of *Abusua*, on one level, that is, that "sub-clan" consisting of the descendants of an ancestor or ancestress to the third or fourth generations, grandparent or great-grandparent. Often, it is the "households" of these more immediate ancestors to which one owes one's societal obligations, primarily, that is, although the collective will of the village or town, the *polis,* in Greek, supersedes that of the "Super-Household." Thus, when a contemporary Akan moves into a relatively more atomized society, as prevails in the West, particularly here in the United States, where such cultural cocatenations border on the outright incomprehensible, if not the outright nonsensical, this is the baggage s/he brings along in contention with all the other pre-Euro-traditional practices encountered in the so-called New World, which by the way, on the threshold of the twenty-first century is still a new frontier to be fully explored, examined and ultimately assimilated. And where the African-American has been described as one possessed of a "double-consciousness," one that is bona fide American, but which is predicated on a culture of moral cannibalism and economic expropriation, and one that is recessively African but irrepressibly militant, the modern continental African may be aptly described as one possessed of "treble-consciousness." On the one hand, is his or her traditional cultural psyche, which has been quite remarkably battered or seriously damaged, such that when the African comes into contact with his or her former conquerors, s/he feels so discomfited as to almost regret his racial identity. Maybe this feeling is what prompted a Ghanaian woman with whom I attended an ethnic-group meeting recently to lament that it was a pity she had not been born white or European. It so happened that an Irish-American woman, we shall call her Naana Donna, was also in attendance. In fact, Naana Donna had even adopted an Akan village where she pilgrimaged at least twice a year, to both initiate and contribute to infrastructural projects. Several years ago, legend has it, Naana had accompanied some Ghanaian friends to Ghana for a two-week vacation and ended up staying for three months. During the course of her stay, she had fallen seriously ill; to her utter shock and dismay, she learned that the nearest health center was some fifty miles away. And even when she finally got there, after a two-and-half hour's ride on a mummy-wagon she had rented, Naana discovered to her chagrin that even such common over-the-counter drugs as Tylenol and Aspirin, were in dire demand. That, in sum, is the story behind the modern health center that now serves the 4,000-plus inhabitants of Akyem-Abenase, in the Eastern Region of Ghana. Shortly after she returned to New York, Naana Donna, who is a senior social worker with the city, organized a few friends and associates and raised nearly $50,000 to start her health-center project. In exchange for her far-reaching beneficence, the chief and people of Abenase invested Naana with the catalytic title of ***Nkosohemaa***, the Queenmother of progress. Of course, some Ghanaians are displeased with the fact that a "common American" white woman, who is not of such "patrician stock" as the Kennedys or the Bushes, would be enstooled as Queenmother. My quick response has invariably been that if all our invested traditional rulers and their ilk could be half as responsible and selfless as Naana Donna, half of Ghana's socio-economic problems would be resolved. Indeed, Naana, by her altruism, gives the lie to mere heredity chieftaincy. Perhaps the entire system of chieftaincy needs a thorough paradigm shift, one that is based more on individual diligence and merit than sheer descent. And on this score, paradoxically, sometimes I feel quite uneasy, particularly when I observe the manner imperial traditionalism seems to be fast creeping onto the American political landscape.

The virtual overnight popularity of Texas governor George W. Bush is one that portends a wrenchingly eerie feeling. The eldest son of former President George H. W. Bush, Junior Bush, the Republican Party's candidate for president of the United States, seems to be coasting towards victory on the flimsy pretext of his father's reputation. For most of us Africans, Ex-President Bush's reputation could not be very enviable. The man served as director of the notorious Central Intelligence Agency (CIA), the institution that is largely responsible for the virtual destruction of the most progressive African leaders over the last forty years—i.e. Kwame Nkrumah, Patrice Lumumba, Joseph Kasavubu, and even Moise Tshombe and Joseph Mobutu Sese Seko.

The Ghanaian lady in question, who wished out loudly that she ought to have been born white, based her tragic conclusion on material reality; which is why even if one vehemently disapproves of her candid confession, one cannot gainsay the fact that every reasonably intelligent person dreams of hobnobbing with winners. Sometimes I dream one of the Williams sisters, the Soyinkas of world-class Tennis, were my girlfriend or companion, though I must also confess that I have one of the most successful continental African women beside me in bed every night. Except, of course, when Oyema kicks me onto the living-room couch from time to time, for the benign crime of snoring the heck out of her calm and quiet. On the other hand, I doubt that any of the winsome Williams sisters had ever wished to have been born white. Indeed, these days of Black domination of golf and tennis, one would rather think that most sport-loving white Americans regret that they had not been born Black or African. What of basketball and the Olympics? Except, of course, one desires to become president of the United States, in which case the least one could be, now that it has become a veritable reality, is Jewish and Orthodox. To most of the so-called mainstream America, which is to imply all white Americans and some honorary Europeanized-Asians, Blackness is the most unorthodox thing to be. Which is why one is apt to think that had Senator Joseph Liebermann, the Democratic Party's vice-presidential candidate for the 2000 elections, been Black his ideological orthodoxy would have meant a double-jeopardy. For many of my fellow continental Africans, both the highly schooled and home-smart, for one is wont to believe that it is only here in America that people could legitimately claim to have been schooled in the streets, the price of whiteness could never be too high. Indeed, so inferiorized have we become that just the other day, a man who had been resident in the United States for nearly three decades confessed to me that he thought the Black man was genetically self-destructive and anti-progress. Adams claims to have been one of the body guards to President Nkrumah at the time of the latter's overthrow. It seems this gentleman has never gotten over the fact that Ghanaians would savagely kill their lone golden-egg-laying fowl. To keep his sanity, Adams has had to reason away the humanity of his compatriots, thereby legitimizing or rather excusing mainstream America's untold brutalities towards the African, both diasporic and continental.

Then of course, the African has had to contend with the debilitating effects of colonialism, which proscribed our very essence and collective self-worth. Not long ago, a Portuguese-Scottish-American woman who had just completed a course in Anthropology, congratulated me on what she deemed to be the auspicious and salutary emergence of Africa from Paleolithic culture into Gatesianism, or cybernetic civilization. I have not spoken to Elena since. Then there was also that white woman who, told that African-American novelist and scholar Toni Morrison had won the Nobel Prize for Literature, sneered at me and exclaimed:

"Impossible! A second Pulitzer, maybe." I would soon discover that in the intricate workings of Affirmative Action, Monica, who earned a little more than I, when I had a master's degree, did not even have a bachelor's degree, though for more than enough number of years for college administrators to have figured out the truth, Monica claimed to have graduated ***summa cum laude*** from the City University of New York.

The greatest impediment facing many a continental African emigrant to the United States is the febrile wish to reap more than we have sown. This problem is the obvious result of grinding poverty, the kind of poverty which Akan legend claims basted the crab and dumped him on the sandy shores of Labadi. Not long ago, a Ghanaian woman who worked as a home-care attendant mysteriously died of Aids. We would learn shortly thereafter that Akosua Mansah had been living high on the proverbial hog. And when a few of her friends and associates politely asked to know how she had come by such lavish existence, being that Akosua officially worked a minimum-wage job, she glibly replied: "My old [white] man looks after me very well." And very well, the old man did! For Akosua Mansah had contracted Aids from the septuagenarian patient she had been professionally assigned to look after.

The treble-consciousness of the contemporary African emigrant to the United States lies in the triple personalities of traditionalism, colonialism and neocolonialism, and assimilationsim. The latter two are interlinked. On the one hand, the recent African immigrant wants to retain his/her African identity. For s/he finds, to her great horror that the phenomenal achievements of the Michael Jacksons, Oprah Winfreys and Johnny Cochrans and Tiger Woodses notwithstanding, the African-American remains pretty much the enslaved and unpropertied underclass s/he has been since the 17th century. In his/her country, the African has been lured into the posh video-display lounges of the U.S. Information Service and bombarded with glamorous servings of James Brown, Muhammad Ali and Andrew Young. If s/he is young, s/he must have seen the rosy, albeit gangster, existence of the rap artists Tupac Shakur, Biggie Smalls, Sean (Puffy) Coombs, Lil Kim, etc.... This might be why these days, my 17-year-old niece dreams of becoming a rap star. Needless to say, I had to join her mother and my other siblings to literally get her butts onto the seat of a college classroom, where she is now majoring in Computer Information Systems (CIS). Years ago, Nana Akua Abasa attempted to enroll into a Dominican gangster group and gave her no alternative but to ship her back home, to Ghana, for a re-education in common sense. Fortunately, it worked. And now Nana Akua is in the top 5-percentile of her college class.

The traditional African in America is blisteringly conflicted. S/he wants to be recognized as a bona fide African, a phenomenon that no longer exists, except in the callow imagination of those who would have the rest of the world believe that precolonial Africa was some Shangri-La. Those among this group who work in the civil service dress beyond "African" recognition during the week. There are some who do janitorial work but dress in three-piece suits like Wall Street bankers. Some among the latter have even been invested as village-heads and chiefs back home. They have managed to scrimp enough to build or buy 2-by-4 homes where they came from; some have also renovated their old, hereditary adobe "palaces." This is the group that Eddie Murphy ought to have consulted before filming his "Coming To America." These "adobe-kings" are weekend traditionalists; they deck themselves in massive funerary clothes heavy enough for ten Muhammad Alis to tote on their pates. It is almost as if they have never gotten over their loss of imperial power during the colonial era, although many of them were unborn, and those among them who were alive were mere toddlers. It is this regressive posse which Nkrumah wanted to run out of Ghana, "with their sandals on their heads." In many respects, they are like the assimilationists, quite thoughtless and stubborn in their silly and stultifying ways. The assimilationists have mastered the kind of idiom that one associates with a piggery, lapping whatever comes their way, indiscriminately, because they were never quite the insiders they now pretend to be of their indigenous cultures. Indeed, they were never quite accepted into the council of dignitaries because their clans and ancestors had been relatively undistinguished. Some of their scion here in America, however, have managed to become diligent, not necessarily very successful lawyers, professors, physicians, bean counters and other professionals and tend to see their remarkable achievements as their own delightful revenge on these societies that refused to recognize them and their kin in high regard. Some have even used their newly acquired status in America to buy such "cheap" titles as "Nkosohene," which they have, in turn, sold to their traditional African culture-enthralled friends, particularly African-Americans, as something to be coveted.

It is in the preceding context, indeed, that the achievements and pratfalls of Ghanaian President Kwame Nkrumah are to be seen. The latter envisaged psycho-cultural and psychical displacement to be the bane of continental African development. Short of any critical or sound transformation in these areas of the proverbial African personality, no amount of material access could turn the massively damaged continent around. It was for this reason that Nkrumah made literacy and constructive education the cornerstone of his development agenda. The pioneering leader in his philosophical classic **Consciencism** (1964), also called for the reconfiguration of a new African, one that appreciated the global and cosmopolitan dimensions of contemporary existence, as well as one that recognized the destiny of continental Africa as one of cross-cultural identification and moral self-revival.

10

Clitoridectomy And African Identity

On March 29, 1997, a Ghanaian woman was arrested at New York City's John F. Kennedy Airport for attempting to enter the United States with forged immigration documents. Adelaide Abankwah, as the woman then called herself and was officially identified as such, would spend the next two years in detention before being released into society, after the vociferous agitation of feminist activists and some American congressional legislators. Among Ms. Abankwah's staunch supporters were the perennial feminist fixture Gloria Steinem and Congresswoman Nita Lowey, of New York State.

It is significant, at this juncture, to observe that the premise for their vocal defense of their ward was that should Ms. Abankwah be returned to Ghana, our protagonist would be summarily subjected to the now-infamous ritual that has become known, largely in Western feminist circles, as Female Genital Mutilation or FGM. That a widely acclaimed scholar and theorist like Gloria Steinem, for only one example, did not conduct even the most routine research that is putatively the indispensable hallmark of scholarship, boggles the mind quite a bit. Unless, of course, one also comes to the realistic acceptance of the fact that most Western liberal, feminist intellectuals and activists are so cynical about the righteousness of their causes that they would stop at nothing to demonize any unsuspecting culture in order to make a point. In this sense, the Western liberal activist is almost invariably ideologically indistinguishable from his/her conservative counterpart, where the "malignant" question of continental African identity is concerned. Just mention the noun "Africa" or its adjectival variation of "African" and every imaginable abomination may be conjured by even the most well-meaning American to shore it up. If the question regards cannibalism, one is apt to evoke the mythopoetic nightmare that was the Biafran War (1967–1970) to establish the putatively unique barbarism of post-colonial Africans.

This author supported the Abankwah episode on totally different grounds—one that was purely political, in the sense of the military-induced economic strangulation of many an African country. That most Africans, as well as most Europeans, Asians, Australians and non-native Americans emigrated from their home-countries for economic and political reasons is quite beyond dispute. And then, in the case of Africans, when one factors in the Western contribution to the perennial economic chaos on the continent, it stands to reason that America should be called upon to redeem its image and leadership by providing succor to the primary victims of neocolonial imperialism. There is apt proverbial observation that it is unwise to spank a child and ask him/her not to cry. For is not the automatic reaction to a spanking a cry?

It may be recalled that at the time of Ms. Abankwah's arrest, many Ghanaian groups and individuals resident in the United States, many of whom are known to have entered the country under equally false pretenses, were up in arms. Some even vowed to attend Ms. Abankwah's judicial arraignment in order to apprise the presiding judge of the fact that the Akan people of Ghana were historically known to be non-practitioners of Female Genital Mutilation. There is the eloquent case of a quite brilliant Ghanaian gentleman who entered the United States on a visitor's visa twenty years ago, from uncompleted studies in an Eastern European nation, and never went back. Some who entered this country just five years ago have even learned how to deliberately injure themselves at work in order to claim permanent or long-term disability compensation.

For this author, any pretext that makes it relatively easy for Ghanaians and other Africans to gain civic admittance into the United States must be eagerly welcomed, all pejorative connotations notwithstanding. For hasn't it been made eloquently clear to Africans, for some four-hundred years now, that to be classified an African in these United States of America is to be summarily proscribed and excluded. And, indeed, it is such rationale that subtends what may aptly be termed the "trickle-down" American immigration policy towards Africa. The only African commodities unreservedly welcome on these shores are African diamonds, gold, petroleum, cash crops and the most highly specialized humanpower resources.

Recently, it has come to public attention that Ms. Adelaide Abankwah's real name (or nom verite) is Regina Norman Danson. Obviously, our protagonist was astute enough to recognize that such a vintage, royalist or aristocratic Western name could not have cut the proverbial ice with the United States Immigration and Naturalization Services (US-INS) had it been cavalierly associated with FGM. Then again, when one looks closely at matters, could one not honestly conclude that the very nomenclatural designation of "the United States of America" is an inimitable fabrication of the first order?

11

Between A Robot And
A Dim-wit

I sketched the outline of this essay on November 9, while attending an annual conference of the Community College Humanities Association (CCHA) in Rockville, Maryland. The latter, as its name implies, is a junior-college faculty clearing house of sorts. "Of sorts" because, by and large, one gets the impression that like its counterparts at various academic and professional levels, CCHA fosters the kind of intellectual masturbation that leaves one wondering: "Am I in the right profession? Or is this whole sociology of knowledge discourse one composed of charlatans and plain-Jane cynics?"

The one significant thing I learned from this conference was not about the conference at all, though it was the "extra-conventional"—no pun intended—theme which dominated the entire two-day confabulation. It was about the just-concluded American presidential and general elections, popularly known as "Election 2000." Nearly three days after the polls closed, the winner of the presidential contest had yet to be declared. The bone of contention was the "Third-World" State of Florida, where both election officials and sizable numbers of the electorate, respectively, weren't either sure of how votes cast ought to be counted and whom they had, indeed, cast their ballots for. Some electors complained that the design of the ballot papers was so confusing that when one entered the polling booth, one could not be certain which voting slot belonged to which candidate.

And, indeed, this confused state of affairs would shortly be confirmed by archconservative, ex-Republican maverick candidate Patrick J. Buchanan, when the latter reportedly received more votes in traditionally democratic districts, which were highly unlikely to have voted for a candidate diametrically opposed to their interests, than in the traditionally, predominantly Republican districts. Mr. Buchanan has been known to make such pathological demands and observations about the purported influx of Africans into the United States constituting the crux of this country's raging economic difficulties, rather than the unhealthy stratocratic budgetary policies of past Republican administrations, particularly the governments of former presidents Ronald Reagan and George H. W. Bush.

Buchanan has also made statements to the effect that U.S. foreign policy is inordinately pro-Israel, while simultaneously claiming that virtually all Arabs are anti-American terrorists and must, therefore, be barred from emigrating to the United States. Mr. Buchanan is not known to have issued any statement regarding the fact that the United States has virtually become a sort of Third Republic of Ireland, the other two being the British protectorate of the Irish Republic and the war-torn, terrorist-ridden and practically colonized Northern Ireland. And the reason is not far-fetched. Mr. Buchanan is an Irish-American.

On the question of the stalemated Election 2000 presidential contest, what many of the CCHA conferees predicted on November 9 as, one would suppose, many other Americans from various walks of life as well, was that it had become evident that the majority of the voting public loved Democratic Party candidate Albert (Al) Gore, thus the latter had aptly garnered most of the popular votes. On the other hand, Republican Party presidential candidate George W. Bush seemed to have locked down the votes of the Electoral College. As it turned out, Mr. Bush, Jr., whose father had stewarded or mis-stewarded America eight years before, depending on the location of a particular critic's sympathies and sentiments, would win the 43rd presidency of the United States, first via a seemingly well-orchestrated fluke of the U.S. Supreme Court, led by its arch-conservative chief, Justice Rehnquist. Republican administrations in the recent past had had the privilege of appointing most of the august Court's constabulary, and so it came as no news that the Court would stop a Florida State Supreme Court-sanctioned electoral recount of ballots cast and declare the dauphin of their most recent benefactor—that is, the majority camp on the Court—winner of Election 2000. Shortly thereafter, the so-called Electoral College of the "U.S. Presidential University" would rubber-stamp the judicial appointment of Texas ranch-recluse George Bush, Jr.

It goes without saying, almost, that the institution of the Electoral College in America's democratic culture is a paradoxical monstrosity because, in the final analysis, it is the general populace whose cause must putatively be championed by the elected president, whose decisions must be deemed to be unimpeachable, not infallible. On this score, one is almost apt to observe that when it comes to the objective practice of democratic culture, either the bulk of Americans are legally blind, or British imperialism never left this side of the Atlantic; it was just that the

Tarquin was run out of town in 1776 by some members of that odious clan who were much more clever than the rest of us as to impose the essential rule of the father on us, without the corporeal presence of the father himself. A Freudian chicanery of sorts.

The whole concept of the Electoral College is one that defeats the purpose of democracy even while vigorously pretending to champion the same. And indeed, contrary to what one might reasonably expect, members of the Electoral College are appointed by the aristocratic echelons of the two major parties, the Republicans and the Democrats, rather than being appointed by the common people, whose interests the august United States Constitution claims the elected should serve. It is a sort of military dictatorship that has managed to finesse a seemingly, chronically confused or weak-minded electorate—and thus preclude the deadly use of artillery—and make-believe the bona fide existence of political freewill. In the process, the general voting public has been hoodwinked into believing that the Electoral College was established by the so-called Founding Fathers to check or arrest the logical, but also seemingly pathological, tendency of the larger states to dominate the process by which the president of the United States is appointed (Terry Moran, ***Primetime Live: ABC-TV*** 11/9/00).

If the preceding assessment has historical validity, then it is obvious that the Founding Fathers lacked even a passable knowledge of elementary Arithmetic, not that it would have mattered anyhow, particularly when one appreciates the fact that "Founding Fatherhood" was not about democracy at all, but rather how to keep the traditional father out of power in order for the rebellious sons to have their own unorthodox ways with the now-unprotected mothers, sisters and daughters of the homestead. This is not a discourse on comparative political systems, just internal logic, so it is not a part of our present purposes to probe the cultural and ideological intricacies of the colonial era of American history. Mathematically, even with the institutionalization of the Electoral College, the larger states still continue to determine the outcome of the presidential selection process. To be certain, the Electoral College is composed of the number of Congressional and Senatorial representation of the individual states constituting the Union; which, in effect, implies that the larger states still field more members or students than the smaller ones. And what is even more disturbing, as one former elector, or graduate, intimated to ABC-TV recently, to be appointed to the College, one must pledge one's immutable non-negotiable acceptance of being used as a political pawn, hence the synonymous designation of "Electoral Pledges." Needless to say, to be designated "a pledge" presupposes one's unconditional acceptance of political sycophancy, a job only worthy of intellectual marionettes than morally responsible citizens. Even some states are known to have passed laws threatening *pledges* who regain the use of their rational faculties in the course of the performance of their duties with jail terms. Such maverick *pledges* are called *defectors*, almost as if it were morally unsound to be conscientious in one's practice of American democracy. Indeed, the preceding might lie behind the reason why the defeated Democratic Party's candidate for president in Election 2000, rather unwisely stated that he would not accept the vote or confidence of a *pledge* appointed by the Republican Party top-dogs to shill for their strong man. And Mr. Gore, who at the time of this writing was substantive vice-president of the United States, through his plethora of public pronouncements, has vehemently registered his utmost displeasure with the institution of the Electoral College. On this score, one may not be presumptuous to question the motives of Mr. Albert Gore, Jr. Either the vice-president is a hypocrite, one who has no deep moral convictions, and thus expects his supporters and the electorate at large not to take him seriously, or Mr. Gore is simply a boldfaced idiot.

While one is wont to concluding that Mr. Gore, like the average politician anywhere in the world, is primarily motivated by opportunism or cynical self-aggrandizement, one can hardly call the former U.S. senator from Tennessee an idiot. The guy is so privileged, and it is interesting to note that Gore's father was also a U.S. senator, like his rival and now President-Elect George W. Bush, that Mr. Gore just doesn't know how best to appropriate his privileged status. Mr. Bush, on the other hand, is Machiavellian enough to recognize raw, brutal power when he sights one in his blood-thirsty crosshairs, and thus almost blandly snatch victory from the proverbial jowls of defeat.

Indeed, if Election 2000 taught those of us who keenly followed events anything at all, it was that stalwarts of the Republican Party, led by their ace "civil rights" activists do not believe in electoral democracy whatsoever. It is not even clear whether these party hacks ever believed in any form of electoral democracy in the past. In all likelihood, these are the reprobate scions of the colonial and ante-bellum Southern planters and fanatical Northern slavocrats. That Mr. James Baker, a professional lawyer and quondam senator, led the judicial effort to stop the Florida vote recount of Election 2000 cold in its tracks is prime grist for dispassionate and objective future historians and political scientists. Mr. Baker, it is interesting to observe, noted in the wake of Election 2000 fiasco that the Gore camp's persistent refusal to accept the results of Florida's electoral fraud, put the country's future on the ominous cusp of anomie. In the final analysis, it was the venerable, elderly British-American Broadcaster Alistair Cooke, in his perennial "Letter From America" (BBC-World Service Radio, 12/25/00) who cast the lackluster tenor of Election 2000 most eloquently. Quoting an unnamed British newspaper on the election, Mr. Cooke noted that Election 2000 was an unfortunate, though not unprecedented, contest "between a brilliant robot and a likable dimwit." Mr. Cooke, however, was perspicuous enough, largely based on hindsight, to also add that such initially underestimated historical figures as Franklin Delano Roosevelt and Mr. Reagan turned out to have been the most outstanding American chief executives of the twentieth century.

12

The Impeachable Rawlings

In the recent run-up to President J. A. Kufuor's official assumption of statutory powers, an agnatic relative of the Ghanaian incumbent quite curiously accused me of being anti-NPP, that is being against the ruling so-called New Patriotic Party and, particularly Mr. Kufuor. Of course, I have written several articles for **The New York Amsterdam News** in the past carping the fact that our protagonist once served under ex-President Jerry John Rawlings, while the latter was ruling de facto as Ghana's "benign dictator," a dubious accolade bestowed by the hacks of the British Broadcasting Corporation's World Service. Whether Mr. Rawlings, the man who meticulously supervised the assassination of three Ghanaian Supreme Court justices, as well as a plethora of other prominent and virtually unknown citizens, deserves to be designated "a benign dictator," is a whole prime grist for future discourse. For now, our spotlight must be trained on the kind of characters that pass for the designation of "leader" in Ghana these days.

While it goes without saying that Mr. Rawlings is almost indubitably the most impeachable president in post-colonial Ghanaian history, it is also significant to appreciate the fact that the shaping of the Rawlings mythology has not been without a whopping dosage of helping from some superannuated members of the extant ruling government including, as aforementioned, President J. A. Kufuor. Indeed, the latter served under Rawlings as minister for local government, for seven months, in the wake of the Rawlings-led putsch that toppled the constitutionally elected Limann administration. In sum, this is why it has become quite difficult for many of us conscientious Ghanaians, both at home and abroad, to accept Mr. Kufuor as a principled, democracy-loving personage. At this juncture, however, it is also significant to appreciate that our aim is not to stipulate that the only characters who are qualified to run the country ought, perforce, to be infallible. Like nationalities all over the globe, ours is not a nation composed of angels or extra-terrestrial beings, or for that matter super-humans. To be certain, this writer served as a student leader, fresh out of high school, under the so-called

December 31ˢᵗ Revolution, an event which many of us have lived long enough to regret and even burlesque. I, however, do not regret my role as a student-leader between 1981 and 1982 with the National Youth Organizing Commission (NYOC), hitherto the National Youth Council (NYC) in Kumasi. Initially, I served as a drama troupe coordinator and helped raise hundreds of cedis in funding for the Ghana Society for the crippled, then headed by Mr. Yaw Attakora, of the Kumasi City Council. I also did a stint at Kajetia roundabout directing traffic and having motorists delightfully throw money at me, as I choreographed my way towards a salutary reduction of gridlock. Earlier, I had also headed the health department of the NYOC, dispatching platoons of students all over the Kumasi municipality to inspect the environmental conditions of restaurants and other eateries and dining establishments, otherwise known as Chop Bars. But, perhaps, I would be best remembered by the genial residents of Kumasi as the first and youngest poet to perform in English, in 1979, at the Ghana National Cultural Center, popularly called Anokyekrom. I did several programs with both GBC-Radio and Television. Most of my presentations verged on the patriotic—i.e. the need to altruistically mobilize the full and total resources of the country in order to make life meaningful for all her citizens. Quite a noble venture, right? Perhaps.

But whether I was successful or not remains to be determined by my peers and posterity. While in Kumasi, as a Sixth-Form student at Prempeh College, and later as a National Service teacher of English, long before I would appreciably master the nuances and intricacies of this colonial heritage, I published three commentary notes on Ordinary Level English Literature (1985–87). It is almost certain that I was perhaps the first non-college/non-university graduate to do so; of course, I had known one or two people, one of them a classmate at St. Peter's Secondary School, who had compiled Objective Questions and Answers for "O"—Level English, largely out of past questions issued by the West African Examinations Council (WAEC). None, however, to the best of my knowledge had assayed the sort of mini-literary treatise that I undertook. Two years after having departed the country, my commentary notes were still being used as curricular staples in some of the major secondary educational institutions, including Ghana National College, in Cape Coast, and Sunyani Secondary School. In both of these government-assisted institutions, the grapevine had it that students who had not purchased my study aids before hand were not being welcomed into their English Literature classes. The titles of my pamphlets were: "Commentary Notes on *A Selection of African Poetry* by Kojo Senanu and Theo Vincent" (1982–1984 and 1985–1987), and "Commentary Notes on Ola Rotimi's *The Gods Are Not To Blame*." At this juncture, I would also like to pay tributes to my parents, the late but still-living spirit of my mother, Dorothy Tomina Sintim (aka Adwoa Attaa Aninwaa and Auntie Attaa), and my father, Kwame Okoampa-Ahoofe, Sr., formerly of the University of Ghana, Legon, and New York City's Technical Career Institutes. It was largely some of the housekeeping moneys that my parents remitted to us, their children, from their sojourn in the United States that I used to produce these pamphlets.

That Mr. Rawlings is appositely impeachable almost beggars debate. The regnant culture of violence is nonesuch in the country's 43-year-old history. Needless to say, somebody has to answer for this culpable trauma and promptly, too. Which means that all the diplomatic pleasantries notwithstanding, accountability and probity ought to be among the top-most agenda of the government of the New Patriotic Party. Indeed, on the occasion of the first democratic transition in twenty years, I listened to an interesting political forum featured by the popular and privately-owned Ghanaian radio station JOY-FM via the Internet. Among the fervid discussants were such young media perennials as Nana Yaa Ofori-Atta, Kwaku Baako, Jr., Kobena Coomson, and Haruna Atta. The program, which I tuned into *medias res*, regarded activities engaged by Mr. Rawlings that could be deemed impeachable offenses. Among the activities enumerated was the merciless and rather savage lambasting of Mr. Arkaah, a Harvard-educated entrepreneur and vice-president during Mr. Rawlings' first elective-term in office. The details of Mr. Arkaah's spanking are murky to this writer at this juncture, but the upshot of it all is the fact that it occurred during a cabinet session regarding an administrative issue. It may be observed that Mr. Rawlings had co-opted Mr. Arkaah's partisan support and deftly maneuvered his way, short of his traditional blitzkrieg method, into legitimacy, in the process of which for electing to play the proverbial devil's advocate and side-kick, Mr. Arkaah had been grudgingly ceded the vice-presidency. In this sense, both Messrs. Rawlings and Arkaah could be fairly characterized as vintage opportunists. Which is not to excuse the curious fact that a police investigation of the case came to naught; this was after it had been eloquently established that Mr. Rawlings had committed a criminally culpable offense. But, of course, the fact that presidential impeachment has never been regarded as a valid entry in post-colonial Ghanaian political lexicon made it plausible that Mr. Rawlings would, literally, get away with murder.

But an even more eloquent prophylactic inhered in the fact that Mr. Rawlings has summarily abrogated our democratic culture and misruled us by the barrel of his gun for a decade, and then finessed his way into electoral legitimacy without having to formally stand down as a military strongman for even one hour, much less one day! Then also, the former president's abuse was remarkably mitigated by the fact that in his blind grab for power, Mr. Nkensen A. Arkaah had reportedly endorsed the flagrant murder of the three Supreme Court justices, and a retired senior military officer, in 1983 as a logical revolutionary fall-out. This is why I, naturally, was amused by the fact that this arguably minor sideshow would be deemed prime grist by the national media in the discourse on our geopolitical destiny.

In this vein, President Kufuor has neither been impressive. In fact nearly two years ago, the NPP chancellor appeared at a forum staged at Hostos Community College of the City University of New York kvetching that a member of the NDC constabulary had accused Mr. Kufuor of owning a Jaguar automobile, a charge that the substantive president, then leader of the organized opposition, vigorously denied. It is interesting to observe that neither President Kufuor's denial nor the aforementioned accusation was worthy of discursive moment of national dimensions. For the issue of interest and concern, as far as the attendees of the forum could envisage, regarded any clear-cut agenda that an NPP government possessed, by way of our collective national reconstruction effort, in the offing. In short, most of the attendees and participants had graced the occasion for communal reasons, only to be rudely and sophomorically subjected to the personal vexations of Mr. Kufuor. I, for one, left the meeting disconsolately daunted, furiously hoping that the tenure of a President John Agyekum Kufuor shall not come to pass. Alas, it has! And this is one reason why I urge my fellow travelers and pedestrians not to hold their breaths or expect any miracles from the Cry-Baby-of-Atwima. I have never trusted die-hard politicians who do not seem to have molded any discrete socially responsible identity short of the hunger and greed for public office. This, nonetheless, in no way implies that able-bodied and "patriotic"—excuse me for appropriating a rather ambiguous and self-serving term—Ghanaian professionals and technocrats, both at home and abroad, ought not throw their full weight behind the NPP administration. What, however, is being herein advocated is that prior to arriving at any such decision, the players involved ought to convince or apprise themselves of the fact that the destiny of our country transcends the interests or aims and aspirations of any particular individual citizen, regardless of social status or ideological suasion.

Furthermore, the rather brazen and insensitive celebration of the so-called December 31st Revolution has been postulated as an impeachable offense; and in many respects it is, particularly when we have been given to understand by the judiciary that celebrating December 31st is extra-constitutional. Hopefully, with the assumption of political reins by the NPP government, December 31st would be promptly and summarily proscribed as a national holiday. Hindsight, needless to say, has proven beyond doubt that December 31st was never about salutary or progressive change, either psychologically or materially, but rather about what may be aptly termed as a "Rawlings Psychosis," a kind of ideological God-complex by which well-intentioned but marginally intelligent individuals undertake, through the application of wanton violence, to reverse the destiny of a body politic, by the unilateral imposition of pseudo-democracy.

Indeed, when Mr. Rawlings vaunts that his nineteen-year reign of terror was about political stability and socioeconomic and moral improvement, one wonders whether the Accra Mental Hospital was not solely established for his cognitive redemption. It is, to be certain, an open secret that the quondam Ghanaian strongman spent most of his tenure simply arming himself and his thugs—the so-called commandos—in order to perpetuate his hang onto power. Today, almost every reputable institution in the country is in a worse shape than it was prior to Mr. Rawlings assumption of office. Ghanaian education, once the pride of the African continent, today is hardly viable. Even university graduates can barely function beyond merely being able to write their names. More than half of my own Ghanaian-educated students at the New York state community college where I have been teaching for the past five years, many of whom graduated from our country's leading polytechnics and teacher-training institutions have had to first enroll in remedial writing courses! I acknowledge with painful humility that when African students in my school have been commended for their intellectual and chirographical acumen, these have often been Nigerian students. Some of my American colleagues, black and white, respond with utmost incredulity when I observe that a graduate of an advanced-level Ghanaian high school holds the equivalent of an associate's degree and sometimes even a little more vis-à-vis the American academic setting. The situation is no better in the health services, transportation and business. In fact, those of us who were old enough between 1979 and 1985 may recall that it was Mr. Rawlings and his (P)NDC government who initiated the systematic destruction of Ghanaian entrepreneurialship. Remarkable numbers of hardworking Ghanaians either had their legitimately acquired property summarily expropriated, or were themselves summarily exiled (and in some cases executed) for owning property at all. Which is why when President Kufuor talks of gainfully resettling his predecessor, many of us believe either Mr. Kufuor is off his rockers, as it were, or the NPP chancellor knows something that the rest of us must crave to learn from him.

It may be legitimate to assert that the very name "Rawlings" is an impeachable offense in Ghanaian statutory lexicon; and we take this opportunity to question the rationale behind the University of Edinburgh's recent conferral of an honorary doctorate on the quondam Ghanaian president, short of the historical fact of Mr. Rawlings' unrecognized patrimony. Or perhaps the "Scottish Harvard" envisages Mr. Rawlings, their neocolonial bastard, as a veritable surrogate missionary in the unenviable project of African political cannibalization? In the final analysis, when Mr. Rawlings arrogantly proclaims, as he did on the eve of his much-welcomed political exit, that: "I am not a friend of multi-party democracy.... It is my honest opinion," perhaps the "deposed" Ghanaian strongman is alluding to something viscerally personal, the fact that he was raised by a single, allegedly promiscuous, mother. There may be something here for future psychologists and psychiatrists to probe and ponder, since it is almost certain that Mr. Rawlings' purported and putative lack of paternal affection and guidance may be central to his publicly intemperate and protracted visitation of misprision on the rest of us.

13

Christianity And Post-Colonial Ghanaian Society

It is often said that the extent and level of the civilization of any society can best be measured by the general manner in which the women of the concerned society are treated by their men. If this observation has any empirical validity, and one would hope that it does, then a recent incident which occurred in a rural Ghanaian community points to the grim fact, or reality, that "civilization" in Ghana is so shallow in depth and breadth that it indubitably leaves too much to be desired. But what is even more confounding is the fact that the advent and infusion of Christian ideological sentiment into the collective Ghanaian national ethos seems to have corrupted, rather than sublimated, Ghanaian moral sensibility. If this latter observation also bears scrutiny or passes muster, as shall be shortly demonstrated, then perhaps the very notion of "modernism" as a hallmark of civic, cultural and technological refinement ought to be thoroughly revised, at least in the realm of basic human behavior.

Early this year (2001), an elementary school teacher in the Western region of Ghana was brought up on charges of statutory rape of seven fifth-graders ranging in ages between 13 and 15 years. In Ghana, this heinous crime was almost casually reported as a traditional case of "seduction," in the Hardian sense. This is not to suggest that most citizens approved of such obviously reprehensible behavior. In the past, the accused, a 32-year-old fifth-grade teacher, would have been summarily ostracized and his family—both nuclear and extended—subjected to public pillory, in the metaphorical sense. And this is why many of us have been dumbstruck by the fact that the administrators of the parochial, Methodist, school in which Mr. John Kofi Bimpong teaches, as well as the top-echelons of the regional and national sectors of the Methodist Church of Ghana, have yet to bring their wayward minion to book or justice. In fact, all reports and evidence point to the culprit being proclaimed a hero, with Mr. Bimpong's most ardent critics being literally branded as traitors to the Christian cause of the Ghanaian Methodism. For not only has Mr. Bimpong continued to teach at the Bogoso Methodist Primary School, but reliable media sources also indicate that the alleged rapist is being assiduously groomed to eventually become an ordained minister of the Church.

Needless to say, the preceding is not without historical precedent. Indeed, it was the norm for much of the nineteenth century, during which period Methodism, and Christianity in general, was introduced into Ghanaian society by British colonial missionaries that Christianity stood head and shoulders above any regnant traditional African religion or brand of ethics. The logic was, therefore, to demonstrate that a conversion to Christianity morally elevated the African convert to the purportedly superior status of an "honorary European." One of the steps towards canonization or Christian refinement was the adoption of a so-called Christian-name at the moment of one's baptism or induction into one of the myriad denominations of the Christian church. Somehow, not "owning" a Christian-name was considered to be an unpardonable act of sacrilege. The "sinner" had no chance of entry into the astral Kingdom of God or Heaven. It was almost as if being born an African was tantamount to being perpetually doomed to perdition. One could only be redeemed by either becoming European or adopting Eurocentric behavior and moral values. The very portrayal of Jesus, the man upon whose purported precepts and livelihood Christianity was ideologically predicated, as a white man, in of itself, pushed logic beyond the realm of reasonable doubt that Africans, in particular, were preemptively mere spectators at the European feast of innate redemption. Indeed, our very colonial existence, a bona fide product of unprovoked European political cannibalization, was pointed to as being symbolic of our primal Christian unworthiness. Of course, since by virtue or vice of our ethnic identity we, Africans, were considered to be scions of Satan-the-detested-outlaw, it only stood to reason that any attempt at our collective destruction by non-African peoples had divine sanction and approbation. Indeed in 1919 after Germany lost in World War I, the East-Indian immigrants of Tanzania and the rest of the East African littoral met in the Tanzanian capital of Dar-es-Salaam to negotiate the colonial expropriation of that African country; it would take the indeflectible brunt of British imperialism to wean the Indians, the traditional colonial surrogates of Britain in Africa, of their rather brazen political initiative.

The need for Christians, and for that matter Christianized Eurocentric Africans, to demonstrate their acquired cultural and behavioral supremacy very much undergirds the decision of the Bogoso Methodist Presbytery and its educational underlings to blindly protect Mr. Bimpong. And here, it is interesting to note that the latter's wife, Adwoa Felicia, one of the nomenclatural anomalies of post-colonial Ghana, is reported to have personally escorted one of the seven teenagers raped by her husband and who got pregnant, to the nearby city of Tarkwa, a renowned gold-mining district, to induce an abortion. Indeed, Mrs. Felicia Adwoa Bimpong's overriding motivation was to stanch any potential marital rivalry, rather than ensure the future well-being of her husband's victim. And the fact that the preceding occurred without the knowledge or consent of the unnamed young woman's parents is quite unsettling, both morally and legally. It seems, interestingly, that the victim's parents were also under the influence and jurisdiction of the local and regional Method establishment, for shortly after pro-testing the carnal violation of their daughter, the pair was reportedly transferred to Kumasi, Ghana's 'second unofficial capital, about one-hundred miles up-country (***Ghanaian Chronicle On The Web*** 2/19/01). We also learn that all the seven sexually deflorated girls, including Mr. Bimpong's primary victim, have since dropped out of school. But what makes these multiple incidents worthy of our serious attention and sustained commentary is the fact of their rampancy and prevalence throughout the country. Indeed, this writer, who was born and raised in Ghana, witnessed several of such incidents, some of them bringing whole com-munities to the brink of rioting.

There is one salient lesson, at least, that the civically-minded observer learns from this harrowing report, and it is that post-colonial Ghanaian Christian ethic is a woefully poor imitation of its non-Christian predecessor and counterpart. And there is almost every reason to believe that as the country has become increasingly Christianized, Ghana has also become intensely corrupt and nihilis-tic. The domination of Euro-Christocentric education has implied that continen-tal African societies begin to seriously consider how to make their relatively, newly-acquired non-indigenous cultures germane to our future destiny. Needless to say, any religious establishment or enterprise that sees the need to defending its central tenets or creed by protecting criminal perpetrators of anti-social behavior is not worthy of judicial legitimacy. In other African countries, such as Nigeria, the bone of religious contention is Islam, not Christianity. In the past quarter-century there has occurred an intolerable spate of carnage, and here specific refer-ence is made to the so-called Kano and Kaduna religious riots, as to sincerely call into question the very proactive concept of "religiosity." In the preceding dis-course, however, our focus has been squarely spotlighted on gender-political imbalance vis-à-vis the cavalier treatment of African women. In the same country (i.e. Ghana), over the course of the last two years, at least 31 women, mostly in their 40s, have been murdered in what some concerned citizens and law-enforcement agents describe as "serial killings" and others term as "ritual murders": all the women victims are also known to be heavy-set. It is also quite curious to learn that most of these deaths occurred under the watch of the just-ousted pseudo-elective monarchy of President Jerry John Rawlings' so-called National Democratic Congress (NDC). The irony is that the immediate former First Lady of Ghana, Nana Konadu Agyemang-Rawlings founded her so-called December 31st Women's Movement in order to fight for gender equity by ensuring the active participation of her fellow country-women in all spheres of national endeavor. Interestingly, on the eve of her stand-down as the de facto premier or doyenne of Ghanaian women, Mrs. Rawlings had yet to utter a word of her view on this heinous crime against Ghanaian womanhood. It is also significant to observe that it was during the reign of the (Provisional) National Democratic Congress (1981–2001) that the hitherto, putative American culture of public gun-toting became a virtual de rigueuer in Ghana. Whether the new civic administration of the New Patriotic Party (NPP) will be able to effectively stanch the high spate of anti-women violence remains to be seen. Thus far, President John Agyekum Kufuor has demonstrated his seriousness in this vein by creating a cabinet-level position dedicated to the developmental affairs of the country's womenfolk. Fighting against the gross abuse of women implies severely punishing the men who make women's societal and moral progress a near-impossibility, and one such prime culprit is Mr. John Kofi Bimpong. Then again, it seems that these days in Ghana all the "Johns" have substantial powers, such as ex-Vice-President John Atta-Mills, ex-President Jerry John Rawlings and incumbent President John Agyekim Kufuor, whereas all the Ms. Xs, the statutorily violated and marginalized, have no legitimate judicial powers behind them, short of the virtually ineffectual rantings of exiled pen-pushers like this writer.

14

Christianity And Africa

"According to a graphic article on AIDS in sub-Saharan Africa in the Feb. 12 issue of *Time* magazine, 'Casual sex of every kind is commonplace. Everywhere there's premarital sex, sex as recreation. Obligatory sex and its abusive counterpart, coercive sex. Transactional sex. Extramarital sex, second families, multiple partners."

The preceding appeared in an Internet report abstracted from the U.S. *National Catholic Reporter* (3/16/01—Accessed 5/29/01). Needless to say, this bestial picture of the proverbially sanctimonious Western Imagination vis-à-vis Africa is simply that, a priggish concoction of a surreal phenomenon purportedly representative of the continental African personality. And it may be further pointed out that this grotesque Western image of Africa is nothing new. It is, however, flabbergasting that even in the "post-civilization era," one may aptly say, little seems to have changed regarding the manner in which the Aryan and Aryanized West continues to envisage global African humanity. And here again, one emphasizes "global African personality" because, invariably, the discourse on AIDS even here in the United States, in particular, and much of the Western world in general, has elected to scapegoat the African-descended person as the vilest form of the human species. And, indeed, so scatological is the general Western-Aryan view of the African personality that on this subject, hardly any perceptible distinctions exist between the attitude of Christians and non-Christians. Interestingly, the former camp often prefers to be perceived as being more morally refined, egalitarian and ecumenical or cosmopolitan in temperament. Fortunately for us, but unfortunately for the very self-righteous Christian West, sizable numbers of continental Africans have been living long enough in this pseudo-cradle of modern civilization, or neo-civilization, to accept such intemperate and scandalous characterization of the African personality without question. Indeed, most of us Western-resident Africans are temperamentally far beyond that reactionary rudimentary or visceral stage of raw outrage at such seemingly unmitigable Western ideological affront at our cultures, persons or personhood and our fundamental, and one may add with apologies to the so-called Founding Fathers of the contemporary American empire, right to exist in God's universe.

Among the Akan of Ghana and the Ivory Coast, and one may quite aptly presume a host of other African ethnic groups and nationalities, there is a common saying that: "Whenever one points an accusing fore-finger at one's target of abuse, or obloquy, the three other fingers point steadily at the accuser." This is a very simple way of saying that people often paint purported portraits of others after themselves, even when such portraits are aimed at eloquently capturing the perceived image(s) of the proverbial "other." This observation may very much explain why I chuckled to myself and said, "This portrait is strikingly American." This comment was more automatic than premeditated; for having being schooled to the highest levels of my discipline as well as nurtured here in the United States over the past sixteen years, I have virtually assumed an American personality, albeit a diasporic African personality. For it is invariably impossible for a non-white person, particularly one of African descent, phenotypically, to transcend the apparently hermetic barrier, what famed and immortalized African-American scholar William Edward Burghardt DuBois characterized "the Veil," that the Aryan mainstream of America has erected to contain non-European peoples. Indeed, this barrier is as imperious and peremptory as the Bible of the American polity, otherwise known as *The Constitution*. It is this document, together with its host of Amendments, that, more than any divine edict, very much determines which resident(s) of these United States must be accorded a privileged status or apotheosized, and which group or individuals condemned perpetually to a miserable state of existence. It just so happens that in the scheme of things, here in the United States, the African-descended person has been virtually and perpetually condemned and consigned to the miserable and abject existence of a non-being. A collective non-being, that is. This disconsolately sorry state was largely what inspired the Black novelist Ralph Ellison to compose his racial epic ***Invisible Man***(1952). Prior to that, the equally inimitable Richard Wright had published ***Native Son***(1940), a novel that caused a lot of controversy between critics who firmly believed that the abject citizenship status accorded the African-American was one that this "jungle-bunny" ought to, at the very least, be grateful for. After all, hadn't Western legend during the course of the last half-millennium institutionalized the execrable myth of the "savage" African graciously brought into the pale of unprecedented enlightenment of Western and American civilization through a purportedly necessary and inevitable process of enslavement?

It is rather ironic to those of us who have been privileged enough to have lived, studied and worked, and even loved, in the Aryanized West, particularly here in the United States, to learn from such polite-society magazine of record as *Time* that "sugar-daddy sex" is intrinsically an African way of life or culture. For starters, however, it is significant to note that the term "sugar-daddy" has no known etymological or linguistic provenance in any known indigenous African language or culture. To be certain, "sugar-daddy" is a term imported into many an urban, continental African culture between the 1960s and 1980s, during the globally explosive era of Discotheques. And unless any honest and objective scholar could explain the preceding otherwise, we almost certainly can confidently reject such Western historiographical mendacity.

As for the characterization of Africans as a people who almost indiscriminately engage in "Transactional sex: sex as a gift," perhaps the least said about this matter, the better. However, if one is correct in interpreting "sex as a gift" as being synonymous with the age-old, global institution of prostitution, then one can reasonably note that the preceding characterization of continental Africans is nothing short of the gratuitous, to say the least. It is almost as if one never heard of the Geishas of Japan, Escort Services in the Times Square environs of New York City, Seattle-Washington, China, India, Thailand, the Netherlands, France and other world-renowned cities and countries too numerous to enumerate. Would the *U.S. Catholic Reporter* quibble over the fact that the euphemism "Red-Light District" is a Western-European parlance or linguistic label, perhaps coined by a distinguished prostitute in London, Paris, New York or Amsterdam? Needless to say, even if we assume that the hideous but very much insistent and imperious institution of "Transactional sex: [or] sex as a gift" is a veritable or bona fide African invention—for, after all, isn't Africa globally regarded as the primal continent?—wouldn't we also be humble, objective and fair-minded enough to recognize the fact that the industrialized and "highly civilized" West has sublimated the culture of "giftable sex" to Shakespearean heights? As for the rather pedestrian, albeit disturbing, fact regarding "premarital sex" and "coercive sex," statistical data on Americans here in the United States, quite to the contrary, indicate that Americans, Christians and non-Christians alike, are among the last of the proverbial Mohicans to wave a morally superior flag at the issue. Indeed not very long ago, on the popular ABC-Television news-magazine "Nightline," a criminal court judge was held up to national scorn and excoriation by Mr. Ted Koppel, host and anchor of the program, because the judge had ordered incriminating signs to be erected on the front lawns of the homes of convicted sex-offenders who had already served their jail terms. Likewise, the commonplace fact that twenty-five percent, or one out of every four, of female American teenagers end up pregnant before their twentieth birthday eloquently rejoins any arguments regarding the purportedly higher moral culture of American youth vis-à-vis their African "peers" and contemporaries.

Indeed, the U.S. Catholic clergy and other church missionaries who composed the aforementioned report on the alleged rampant sexual abuse of African nuns by African priests and other highly-placed church officials, were sophisticated enough to also note that the disturbing problem of casual sex in the Age-of-Aids is not peculiar to the African continent. However, so half-hearted is such observation that, aside from its unmistakably brazen hypocrisy, such statement of apparent dispassionate mitigation ends up actually depicting African sexual habits as uniquely bizarre. One paragraph from the U.S. **National Catholic Reporter**, for example, reads: "Even accounting for promiscuity—which in fact, some experts have argued, is no less a problem in Western nations—the religious men and women raising the issue of sexual exploitation of religious women say the situations they report on are clearly intolerable and, in some cases, approach the unspeakable." And "intolerable" it well should be deemed. For the descriptive of "religious" glibly used to characterized glaringly perverted Satanists, especially if one strictly casts the issue and situation in Christocentric terms, scandalizes the term itself. It is also significant to point out that readers are not told that Western priests might be involved in the wanton abuse of the African nuns. Historically, European missionaries and colonial personnel who sexually exploited African women were never punished or disciplined, except, perhaps, in rare cases and circumstances. Oftentimes, to be certain, these scoundrels were even reassigned plum positions which virtually amounted to professional promotions. For, in reality, European missionaries and conquerors in Africa never regarded their untold crimes against African humanity and the continent in general as any crimes at all; at the worst, such crimes as were committed against Africans come to be regarded as mere misdemeanors. One only needs to read Joseph Conrad's liberal classic **The Heart of Darkness** (1924), for a fuller appreciation of this problem.

Thus in all the preceding, the problem at stake is less the wanton abuse of African nuns by male priests and other church officials, than the historical temperament or attitude of the Church towards the African people. Indeed, the avid student of African literature knows of such wanton cases of abuse from reading novelists like Mongo Beti, in the Cameroonian author's satirical picaresque **The Poor Christ of Bomba** and, regarding the abuse and exploitation of Africans by Europeans, from another versatile Cameroonian novelist and politician Ferdinand Oyono's **Houseboy**. So depraved has been the role of the Roman Catholic Church in Africa, particularly with regard to the summary enslavement of Africans, that in 1981, while on an official visit to Ghana, Pope John Paul II literally kissed the soils of that African country concomitant with profuse apologies, in hopes of redeeming or reconstructing the indubitably tainted image of the Church in the African mind. Whether the Pope succeeded in whitewashing the Church of Rome before the African Gods may be deemed moot, the much-touted beneficence of the Church to Africa, in material terms, of course, notwith-standing.

Indeed, what is most painful to Africans, both on the continent and in the diaspora, to having Western do-gooders and "experts" hang their proverbial dirty laundry out to dry in the public square, is that oftentimes such exposes are conducted with no intent of facilitating a salutary remediation. In other words, for most Africans, it is almost as if Western scholars, leaders and experts have nothing constructive to offer the continent and her peoples short of perpetually holding us to scorn. Thus, for instance, President Thabo Mbeki was called to the carpet by Western governments and reporters, because the South African premier had intimated that the perennial scourge of grinding poverty was more devastating to the continent than the Aids pandemic. While it could reasonably be concurred that Mr. Mbeki had naively and rather unrealistically elected which pressing African problem deserved prompt or immediate attention, it is also interesting to observe that most of his ardent critics had not suggested, in material terms, how to constructively assist a debt-ridden continent to overcome a veritable state of crisis threatening the very foundations of its existence. All that these critics seem to expect of Mr. Mbeki and, indeed, many an African leader, was for them to simply and fatuously agree with their supposed Western moral superordinates that Africans were to blame for the outbreak and rapid spread of Aids. And here, it goes without saying to note that the funerary acknowledgment by African leaders, of diverse ideological bents or suasions, since the dawn of political autonomy has not rushed a single European nation or government to the continent to help develop viable and strategic solutions to her myriad problems, most of which are problems created by Western colonialism. The psycho-cultural damage to the continent and the African personality by Western colonialism has virtually gone unrecognized by experts of the erstwhile colonial powers. Even when recognized, the diagnosis has almost invariably been one of victim-blaming. Indeed, the very human intellectual capacity and capabilities of the African continues to be held suspect. And when grudgingly recognized, it has been to credit the erstwhile colonial master with being responsible for creating a nurturing environment for such enviable African achievements. Thus in 1986, when Nigerian playwright, thinker and human rights activist Wole Soyinka was awarded the Nobel Prize for Literature, some cynical British commentators were to be heard on BBC World Service radio touting the fact that Mr. Soyinka was educated by Britons, both in Nigeria and the United Kingdom. The fact that the formerly colonized and culturally cannibalized African had also remarkably contributed to the development of British and European cultures in all fields of endeavor over nearly half-millennium was never seriously raised as a significant discursive subject.

In the final analysis, it cannot be gainsaid that the twenty-first century demands, cross-culturally and globally, that we become better human beings and our proverbial brothers' and sisters' keepers. From the preceding, it does not appear that religion—be it Christianity, Islam, Hinduism, Sikhism, Traditionalism—has helped us very much to recognize our common identity and destiny. Indeed, if anything at all, it appears that denominational religion has grossly facilitated global humanity's alienation from one another, all sanctimonious ideological pretension to organic pacifism notwithstanding. Nonetheless, the imperative need for global humanity to forge a salutary culture of proactive interdependence is one that cannot be ignored. The survival of the world in the decades and centuries ahead depends on our egalitarian collaboration, what some leaders of foresight have aptly termed as "partnership," as distinguished from the current "horse-rider" relationship. We cannot afford to lose.

15

Anatomy Of The African Mind

Not quite long ago, an interesting newspaper article titled "Africa Still a Frontier for Slavery" appeared in the New York *Daily News* (May 7, 2001: 17). Written by African-American columnist Karen Hunter, the article reported civil rights activist Alford Sharpton's then-recent return from a fact-finding visit to the northeastern African country of the Sudan. The renowned activist had toured the Arab-dominated country in order to investigate widespread reports regarding the soul-cringing prevalence of slavery. After dispiritingly satisfying himself that indeed, slavery did exist in the Sudan, Ms. Hunter reports that the good, old ordained Baptist minister without a chapel fumed with utter disappointment: "Whether it's blacks enslaving blacks, or whites enslaving blacks, slavery is wrong." The flamboyant and pontifical preacher added: "The objective [of abolishing slavery] was never to replace [white with black] slave masters, but to have freedom" (latter brackets appear in the original).

Needless to say, it is quite ironic but understandable that Sharpton, from his Eurocentric stance or perspective in the West, should erroneously assume that the institution of slavery, with the African human as the sole commodity of trade, is a bona fide European invention, perhaps even invented in the United States by the notorious, incurable race-profiling white man. And while it is quite refreshing to hear such a publicly vocal personage of Rev. Sharpton's caliber decry contemporary slavery in continental Africa, it comes almost as a grim and total surprise, in some respects, that Mr. Sharpton should have waited for so long to acquire such remarkably grave but beneficent perspective on the issue. In a sense, our genuine surprise may be reasonably answered by the fact that the veteran, third-generation civil rights champion is not your traditional African-American intellectual at an urban public college or university. In fact, the last classroom desk at which Mr. Sharpton sat was in high school. Which, in fact, is not a winning riposte to his having been too long in the dark about slavery in Africa, particularly as it prevails in the Sudan. To be certain, the first leading Afrocentrist to raise the question was

Temple University's Molefi Kete Asante, in his 1992 anthology of essays titled *Malcolm X and Other Afrocentric Essays* (Africa World Press). For the most part, many of the leading African-American intellectuals and scholars have stayed clear of the matter, particularly African-American writers and journalists of Islamic persuasion. Consequently, it came as quite a surprise when this writer read the *New York Amsterdam News'* version of the Sharpton trip to the Sudan (April 19-26, 2001). The article, which appeared with a banner headline on the front page of the preceding weekly, magisterially titled: "Sharpton's Mission: Anti-Slavery Crusade Takes Sharpton to Sudan" was written by ace freelance reporter and Afro-Islamic nationalist Yusef Salaam. The surprise was more about the writer of the said *Amsterdam News* article than about the continent. Unless, *Amsterdam News* readers have extremely short memory banks, of course. For about ten years ago, Mr. Salaam, who also happens to be a dear friend and colleague of this writer, made a tour of the Sudan and cheerfully reported, amidst deafening fanfare and absolute contempt for his opponents on the issue, that Sudan's much-touted contemporary culture of slavery was a sheer figment of mainstream, anti-Islamic American imagination. At the time, this writer questioned the rather blasé manner in which Mr. Salaam was defending the Sudanese government. And here, I am humble enough to admit that I stood at a woefully disadvantageous position, since I had not and still have not been to the Sudan. Of course, the next time I meet with Mr. Salaam or happen to give my dear friend a courtesy call, I intend to remind my "Muslim Brother" that one cannot talk from both sides of one's mouth, as it were.

Like almost every significant Western leader, regardless of ethnicity, racial identity or political persuasion, Rev. Sharpton, understandably, has been deeply engrossed in the behemoth and myriad problems of Black America, particularly vis-à-vis mainstream America's institutionalization of racism, a phenomenon that borders on abject and summary proscription of the African-descended American, to be too concerned about *l'Affair d'Africain*. And to be certain, the abolition of slavery in the United States as well as the stanching of its efflux in Africa, was not about Africa at all. It was primarily about an embarrassed self-righteous industrializing West modernizing its economy, as well as morally seeking to indemnify itself. And, in fact, even during the colonial phase of the proverbial African experience, the West paid scant attention to the expropriation, degradation and outright dehumanization of the indigenous African personality. In the Sudan, for example, as in many other countries on the continent, Afro-Arab destruction of Africans was allowed to proceed, so long as these Muslim Arabs were not seen to be undermining the imperialistic intentions of the Western powers. In the process, as Asante quite eloquently adumbrates (see ***Malcolm X and Other Afrocentric Essays***), the British, by the close of their colonial governance in the Sudan, had created two societies, a virtual hostage polity in the predominantly indigenous South, and the supercilious captor or domestic imperialist North. This carcinogenic state of affairs very much explains the perennial civil war raging in the Sudan. And the fact that other relatively more liberated countries on the continent have been plagued by weak-willed leadership, or near-total absence thereof, has not meliorated the situation. An Nkrumah, for example, would have squarely taken up the issue and dealt justice to it, although one could almost be certain that this would not have been in the interest of the erstwhile Western imperialist powers who seem to be perpetually poised to dominating and regressing the developmental prospects of post-colonial Africa.

As aforementioned, African-American leadership has been too deeply swamped by the complex psycho-cultural and economic difficulties of Black America to be an effective force in the affairs of the proverbial "Motherland." Not at least in the manner by which the United States, through the global workings of the North Atlantic Treaty Organization (or NATO) has been able to exert quite a profound influence over the destiny and internal affairs of the so-called European Community. Needless to say, here in the United States, the diasporic African personality has yet to fully emerge as a political force to be reckoned with by the mainstream of society, short of the largely thespian quadrennial electoral minstrelsy.

The preceding notwithstanding, the genetico-cultural assumption of Africanity by the diasporic Black person in America has also implied, at least at the emotional and moral levels, the inevitable global burdens and responsibilities that come with being an African. For being an African is primarily a socio-economic construct. Thus, it did not come as much of a genuine surprise when in the early 1990s, a survey conducted among Black people in America indicated that only a third of these continental African-descendants concurred with the geocultural or political label of "African-American." The rest of the two-thirds majority wanted little or nothing to do with the preceding label. Thus, it would be quite accurate to characterize the atmosphere of the early 1990s, when the Reverend Jesse Louis Jackson "mainstreamed" the ethnic descriptive of "African-American" as an era of at best woeful cultural ambivalence and at worst outright racial self-hatred among African-Americans. Back then, even Mr. Jackson described American Blacks as a people in whose veins coursed two main blood-types; one blood-type was African, and the other European. For Mr. Jackson, it seems, his putative European blood-type was as significant as his institutionally recognized and incriminated

African blood-type. Perhaps, the precocious and ace civil rights firebrand activist had figured that with time the proscribed European blood-type of the Black American would be duly and legally recognized. Sad to confess, the latter has yet to occur. And the situation does not seem to be getting any better; indeed, every four years, Black candidates for president of the United States get invariably asked in the third-person: "What does Jesse want?" "What does Keyes want?" "What does Fulani want?" Even at the mayoral and senatorial levels, except for the pioneering Mayor David Dinkins, African-Americans often get questioned about their "vaulting" ambitions, in raw Shakespearean parlance, for rights and privileges that members of other races, including even some who are considered racial and ethnic minorities, take for granted.

For the most part, the rather tragic refusal of the collective self-acceptance on the part of Black Americans, particularly those who consider themselves to be squarely situated among the noble ranks of the so-called Talented Tenth, has, largely, to do with the abject historical memory by which things African have come to be associated with right here in the United States. The image of Africa as portrayed in novelist Alice Walker's Pulitzer Prize-winning epistolary fiction **The Color Purple**, for instance, is quite gratuitous and almost ahistorical; it is one of abject betrayal of kinship trust, continental and global African kinship, forgetting the historical fact that "Blackness" as a viable or practical ideological label is a purely Western manufacture. Nonetheless, it is quite understandable that in both the novel and the movie, one character is seen and heard lamenting to another roughly thus: "Our African kin, we are told, sold us into slavery for crimes committed against African societies. Even if our ancestors had committed such heinous crimes as attributed to them, why couldn't they have been punished in Africa, where these alleged crimes were committed?"

Of course, the preceding is a rather long-winded and embarrassingly prosaic paraphrase of the much more felicitous original. Nevertheless, it reasonably encapsulates the gist of the indubitably psycho-culturally wrenching implications of the African-American experience, particularly among the diasporic African elite who have often minced no opportunity in roundly castigating their continental African kin, whose epic memory regarding the intricate dynamics of the so-called Trade in African Humanity, it is significant to observe, is often as hazy and sketchy as that of the African-American. And indeed, the results or after-effects of our mutual and collective enslavement and dehumanization by the West, and ourselves, has been unmitigably withering and stultifying on both sides, with descendants and citizens on both divides of the Atlantic Sisyphically struggling to rationalize and come to terms with this most untenable of crimes against humanity.

Unfortunately, in recent times, on the American or diasporic African side, it has become fashionable for the average college-educated person or intellectual, the so-called middle-class, of whose upper- or lower-classes one is often quite uncertain about, to envisage his/her relatively more materially "improved" conditions as condign revenge upon his unmitigably treacherous continental African kin. Some prominent African-American literary figures have even been recorded as claiming little or no affinity, whatsoever, with continental Africans. Famed novelist Richard Wright, for example, may be aptly observed as one significant case in point.

In his equally equivocal and self-congratulating travelogue masquerading as authentic and radical African history, ironically titled **Wonders of the African World** (Alfred Knopf, 1999), renowned Harvard University scholar Henry Louis Gates, Jr., recalls an instance in Richard Wright's wanderings, during a "homecoming" visit to Ghana in the late 1950s, when the immortalized writer had the prime opportunity to, as it were, get back at the descendants of the traitors and sellers of Wright's forebears and ancestors. Unsurprisingly, Gates portrays Wright's Ghanaian hosts as total imbeciles. These rather uncommonly genial hosts, indeed, had made the mortal mistake of reaching out warmly to their "returnee kin," by heartily remarking on Wright's striking resemblance to native West Africans. Here, Gates almost doubles up with laughter by relating to spectators and readers that to the rather curious and purely innocent question: "Did your grandparents not inform you of which part of [West Africa] your ancestors came from?" the irrepressibly enraged Wright vitriolically snapped: "You know, the white men to whom your ancestors sold my ancestors did not keep any records of our origins? Did you?" That Professor Gates waxes with glaring amused contempt as to rather immodestly gloat over this purely human and humane act of prized kinship proffered amidst epistemological ignorance and confusion, almost certainly detracts from the author's integrity as a self-avowed scholar of African literature and history. To the renowned Harvard professor, therefore, Wright was the wit, even as the latter's Ghanaian hosts pathetically confirmed themselves to be abject fools for the encounter. Does it therefore come as any **wonder** that Mr. Gates' **Wonders of the African World** has been widely denounced by many progressive African-American scholars and their continental African counterparts as a nonesuch farce, an outright burlesque, even as some misguided African and African-American intellectuals have also unreservedly lauded both the book and the movie for "telling it like it is." For instance, Professor Wole Soyinka, far and away Africa's foremost dramatist and a formidable political activist and critic, has come out in staunch support of this Gatesian hatchet job. This is hardly surprising, for both the movie and the book versions of Gates' **Wonders of the African World** were partially dedicated to Mr. Soyinka. Interestingly, Mr. Anthony Kwame Appiah, a Harvard professor of African Literature and Western Philosophy—currently chair of African-American Studies at Princeton University—and staunch colleague and bosom friend of Gates', to whom went the other half of the Gatesian dedication, has remained remarkably silent on the issue, at least up to the time of this writing.

Perhaps with some justification, Mr. Soyinka has vehemently defended his ward, his long-lost academic and diasporic nephew, against the caustic criticism of Professor Ali A. Mazrui, the pioneering African political historian and the first continental African to undertake a major bibliographical and filmic survey of the primeval continent (see **The Africans: A Triple Heritage.** Boston: Little, Brown, 1986/BBC-TV), for what the Nigerian playwright and Nobel literature laureate terms as Mazrui's self-serving criticism. In his rejoinder to Professor Mazrui, whose filmic survey on Africa Professor Soyinka termed as "a half-way house," the versatile literatteur, himself an authoritative teacher and critic of African literature and Mr. Gates' mentor at Cambridge University, accuses Professor Mazrui of brazenly "pleading his own cause."

In the final analysis, the fact that the preceding and, almost, every single significant cross-Atlantic or global discourse between Africans and African-Americans is unmitigably and invariably mediated by the common dilemma of our slavo-colonial experience is often either inadequately considered or even totally overlooked. Even where any semblance of recognition is accorded, this is invariably glancing or so bland as to be deemed tantamount to outright non-recognition. Not infrequently, interlocutors on both sides, quite inadvertently, assume the deleterious consequences of our enslavement and colonization for their causes. In the process, the discursive insensitivity becomes internecine, with some continentals gloating over the purely accidental fact that their ancestors had not been deported to the Americas, often forgetting that the mere non-shipment into the Americas did not necessarily imply non-enslavement on the native continent itself, which is not morally significant at all, especially when one reckons the fact that regardless of its perceived benignity or malignity, the status of slavery is never one of privilege. Sometimes out of embarrassment, on the part of continental Africans, that is, the riposte has blandly been that: "One does not sell one's prime turkey or the hen that lays the golden eggs for nothing, or no good reason at all." The "something" of implicit African-American culpability in their own enslavement is, however, hedged around or conveniently skirted. For there is no justification, whatsoever, for continental Africans' complicity in the abject enslavement of their African kin, the disparate historical concept or understanding of ethnicity and nationality notwithstanding.

On the other hand, while for the most part progressive African-American intellectuals and scholars are generally conciliatory towards their continental kin, like the latter, there is also the tentative feeling of moral superiority, the kind of moral superiority that Holocaust survivors and other targets of Nazification are purported to wield over their enemies. However, unlike its retributive Jewish version a la Nuremburg, and other subsequent search-and-destroy missions against escaped Nazi culprits, at worst African-American moral superiority has been expressed in a paradoxical manner that seeks to justify the material benefits of contemporary American society and, by extension, Black America by envisaging the heinous crime of African enslavement almost as a blessing in disguise. Indeed, even Kenyan scholar Ali A. Mazrui in his aforementioned book *The Africans: A Triple Heritage* (1986), seemed to celebrate the fact that the enslavement of continental Africans brought us into the supposedly auspicious ambit and orbit of Western globalism. For his part, when he returns to the United States upon the completion of the film version of *Wonders of the African World*, Professor Gates would muse to his audience that he felt privileged to have descended from enslaved Africans, because the contemporary material conditions on the continent rendered the African rather too "primitive" (implicitly, of course) for the African-American to feel any pride in being affianced to the proverbial beggarly, or mendicant, "Ethiopian Brother" of Western Band-Aid mythology. Elsewhere, Gates would tentatively claim, almost without any attempt at goodwilled self-refutation that African-Americans are so profusely talented in ways that continental Africans have not been known to be endowed, for the former to seriously crave any meaningful kinship with the latter.

That such callow and clearly gratuitous and ahistorical pronouncements should come at a time when sizable numbers of cross-Atlantic or global Africans are seeking reparations for the horrid crimes against their humanity by the Aryan West, over the last half-millennium, is strikingly ironic and interesting. Needless to say, Mr. Gates over a decade ago firmly established his stature and integrity as a studious and diligent savant of African-American Studies, with such innovative critical works as *Figures in Black* and *The Signifying Monkey*; all of which implies that the West Virginian native, as he exults in being called, in reality, did not need this recent misadventure into his so-called *Wonders of the African World* to further boost his professorial image or scholastic stature. If the preceding, indeed, approximates his intent, then Mr. Gates woefully and eloquently failed on both fronts, which is a very sad commentary on his otherwise brilliant academic career. Even while one may not agree with much of Gatesian scholarship and, to be certain, this is no original or profound statement, it is almost universally agreed upon that Professor Henry Louis Gates, Jr., is an academic workhorse, where many of his colleagues and adversaries, particularly those on the so-called ideological Left, may be aptly seen to be more demagogic than scholastic.

The preceding maugre, it may not be far-fetched, indeed, to suggest that the entire Gatesian project, as manifested by the so-called **Wonders of the African World**, was deftly orchestrated to stymie the ongoing discourse on global African reparations. For the definitive statement or theme underlying *wonders* is one that impugns the legitimacy of the aforementioned discourse. Thus *wonders* may be seen to squarely undermine the cross-Atlantic, collective self-confidence of Africans and consequently facilitate the perpetuation of their current and seemingly perennial subjection to the Western, imperialist geopolitical and cultural status quo. Which may be why here, in the West, Africans have almost uniquely been depicted as the only people who sold themselves into slavery, and therefore a people in no way deserving of international or global sympathy, the way Nazified Jews and European Gypsies have been envisaged over the past half-century. On this score, even such sacerdotal accounts as the Bible's on the morally universal question of slavery have been summarily discounted, in favor of maligning the proverbial "Mother" of all scapegoats in the modern era, the global African personality. Furthermore, the fact that to-date not many voices have been equally raised against the known and abject complicity of some ethnic Jews in the Nazi Holocaust must pique the interest of all well-meaning people, Jews included. Needless to say, we point out the preceding merely to underscore the fact that the tragic phenomenon of African enslavement and psycho-cultural and physical destruction is as worthy of as much moment or attention as any other calculated acts of expropriation and proscription. Thus, just as the need to remedy the Nazi holocaust against the Jews has been globally recognized as a matter of course, or routine, in the incontestable context of basic human decency, the holocaust of African enslavement must be recognized as such.

But perhaps the most significant observation on the question of slavery, freedom and reparations was best made by African-American journalist Karen Hunter. In the latter's article quoted at the beginning of this essay, Ms. Hunter poignantly notes: "This recent recognition of slavery in Africa is not about race or color. It is about a mentality—the same mind-set that allows slaves to be held in

Africa by Arabs and Africans is what allowed slavery, Jim Crow and racial profil-
ing to exist here [in the United States]. It is the [grim and bewildering] notion
that another human being is somehow less intelligent, less worthy of human[e]
treatment. And until that mentality is abolished[sic], there can be no forgetting
or getting over slavery in this country or abroad.... Before we can free anyone
from physical bondage, there must be a concerted effort to change how we think
about one another" (New York **Daily News** 5/7/01:17). Sorry to say, white-
America does not seem to have remarkably altered the way it thinks about black-
America, in particular, and other politically categorized racial minorities, in general. Which is why when Ms. Hunter cautions that: "If black Americans and
Americans in general cannot care about the plight of slaves in Africa today, we
may not have evolved very far from the culture that allowed the transport of tens
of millions of Africans to these shores for free labor and worse."

And to be certain, we have not evolved very far from the ideological mind-set
of those who we arrogantly prefer to describe as "our primitive ancestors." If anything at all, among African-Americans we may be ominously devolving into a
state of indescribable decadence, as we frenetically crawl over one another in our
apocalyptic rush to assimilating into the proverbial American national prejudice.
The contemporary diasporic African personality is, without great exaggeration,
almost entirely composed of self-righteous bigotry. Thus it is quite interesting to
observe that while their nineteenth-century predecessors—among them Delaney,
Crommell, Blyden, Walker, Allen, etc.—were vigilant and astute firebrand fight-
ers and activists against African proscription and routine enslavement both on the
continent and in the Americas, late twenteith-century African-American leaders
by and large, with remarkably few exceptions, merely seem to wax blasé about
momentous and catastrophic events on the cradle continent. Thus, one does not
infrequently read of a Roy Innis, a Jesse Jackson or a Louis Farrakhan consorting
with such reprobate African dictators as Sani Abacha, Jerry John Rawlings, Ibrahim Babangida, Muammar Khadafy, Omar Bongo and Jammeh, without any of
these avowedly ardent enemies of autocracy raising any significant concerns about
the virtually stultified and outright frozen fate of the masses of Africans over
whose precarious existence these strongmen comfortably repose.

Indeed, it is no accident that this ludicrous state of affairs has prevailed for
almost as long as direct colonialism has ceased to exist on the continent. First of
all, and this is a rather tragic commentary on our leadership integrity as a people,
African-Americans having been almost pathologically imperialized by slavery and
internal colonialism, otherwise known as Jim Crowism, have almost perfectly
assumed the very guises of the political overlords whose reign of terror they have

detested and vigorously fought against for at least three-hundred years. No wonder, then, that prominent but "mainstreamed" Black leaders and politicians like Colin Luther Powell and Condoleezza Rice, among a myriad of others, have tended to envisage themselves first and foremost as ***Americans*** or implicitly ***Afropeans***, that privileged species of African that would rather summarily forget the tragic African past and all kinship ties to the continent so as to freely relish the wanton fruits of capitalism with little or no remorse. For this species of leader, Africa is as emotionally and psychologically surreal as life on the Arctic or Antarctica. Africa merely exists as an escapable myth whose ignominy renders it apt to be consigned into perpetual oblivion. In short, to this breed of African-American leader, Africa does not exist; only the ***Black South*** exists, and the genetic affinity of this ***Black South*** to Africa is at best irrelevant, epistemologically or historically speaking. At the other end of the spectrum, we have such interesting and morally conflicted characters as Stanley Crouch, Shelby Steele, Orlando Patterson, Thomas Sowell and Keith Richburg. Needless to say, it is against such withering ideological bottlenecks that the fiercest battle for global African liberation will be fought. Of course, the list is hardly exhaustive for both African-America and continental Africa.

16

Mixing Apples and Oranges

While the Israeli-Palestinian dilemma continues to agonize most well-meaning people all over the world, some cynics have sadly assumed that cavalier and disingenuous stance of expedient comparatists. But whether such paralogical approach to ethics passes muster in the long run remains to be seen. The latest serving of the preceding order appeared in a rather pathetic plaintive in *The New York Times*' Week in Review issue of August 4, 2002. Bylined Richard Bernstein and titled "An Ugly Rumor Or an Ugly Truth?" the article sought to vindicate the Israeli response to the Palestinian question. However, what piqued my quizzical interest as an African was the lame attempt by the author to equate the much-criticized activities of the Israeli government with the, admittedly, equally grim state of affairs in Central Africa, particularly in Rwanda and the Congo.

To be certain, Mr. Bernstein had no need to engage in linguistic floridity or ideological pyrotechnics; that had already been deftly done by the editors of *The New York Times*, who placed the nightmarish picture of some exhumed skeletal remains from the Rwandan genocide of 1994 below Mr. Bernstein's tirade. The suggestion was not farfetched—the reported killings by Israeli soldiers of Palestinian civilians last spring in the West Bank town of Jenin was sheer concoction; if one wants to know just what and how a real massacre looks like, the picture seems to say, one ought to visit Rwanda. But, perhaps, since the average reader may neither have the time nor the wherewithal to so, we (the magisterial editors of *The New York Times*) thought it quite apposite to provide you, our loyal reader, with a graphic and classical example of genocide.

At the end of the article, Mr. Bernstein seems to argue why widely reported Israeli atrocities against Palestinian civilians ought to be regarded as pedestrian or sheer propaganda. To this effect, the well-known book critic writes: "Indeed, the death toll in the most recent Israeli-Palestinian conflict, which began in September 2000, is just 2,000 people, roughly 1,500 of them Palestinian. That is a far lower number than in most of the world's conflicts, and a fact that makes condemnation of Israel in Europe seem all the more disproportionate."

In the preceding, it is not clear whether Mr. Bernstein is implying that until Israeli soldiers kill at least 6 million Palestinians, like the Nazis did to European Jewry, the whole world should keep silent and pretend that the internecine conflict raging between Israel and Palestine is just another friendly meet at a ball game. But what is even more significant, which the writer fails to point out, is the fact that the United Nations' investigation or inquest into the alleged Jenin massacre was methodically stage-managed by Washington and Tel Aviv, in such a manner as to leave one wondering what would have become the fate of Hitler and his infamous SS, if the latter had had a champion in Washington or Moscow to facilitate a deft and swift downplaying of the grim realities of Auschwitz. For starters, it is significant to recall that a timely team of expert investigators dispatched to Jenin by United Nations Secretary-General Kofi Annan was rudely prevented from undertaking its fact-finding mission, on the rather specious and risible grounds that the august world body lacked the requisite objectivity and credibility for such purpose.

The preceding notwithstanding, it is also interesting when Mr. Bernstein instances Rwanda and Congo as eloquent pretext for normalizing Israeli government atrocities against the Palestinians. To this effect, he writes: "For example, Rwanda and Congo have just signed a treaty that may end their war of intertribal slaughter. Hundreds of thousands of people have died, but at no point have editorial writers like Mr.[A.N.] Wilson "reluctantly suggested that those countries should no longer exist." Needless to say, I invite Mr. Bernstein to read the massive literary corpus of late Ghanaian president Kwame Nkrumah regarding the need to reconfigure the geopolitical realities of post-colonial Africa and report back to his readers in short order. Indeed, it seems that beyond the vapid offerings of *The New York Times* on Africa, and the rest of the so-called Third World, in general, all that Mr. Bernstein reads is himself. And this is a great pity.

Three years ago, when Godfried Schonfeld of the Jewish Commentary vitriolically attacked me in *The New York Times* for daring to present a scholarly paper titled "When Human Dignity Is Besieged: An Afrocentric Critique of the Diary of Anne Frank," at a Holocaust scholars' conference, I solemnly promised myself never again to write on any issue pertaining to Israel and the Palestinians. Unfortunately, the persistent attempt by Mr. Bernstein and the editors of *The New York Times* to use Africans as punching-bags to further their own side of the Middle-Eastern question, has forced me to speak to this tabooed topic. I hope my admirers, and even my enemies, would forgive me for this breach. I just could not help myself; for as my Presbyterian clerical, maternal grandfather used to say: "Plain talk purges the soul."

II

Richard Bernstein's article titled "An Ugly Rumor Or An Ugly Truth" (*New York Times*/Week In Review, August 4, 2002:14) is seriously undermined by the author's attempt to equate Israeli government-sponsored atrocities against the Palestinians with the Rwandan civil war of 1994. For starters, the writer complains bitterly about what Mr. Bernstein believes to be the virtual silence of European critics of the Sharon government on the Rwandan-Burundian genocide. Interestingly, the writer also fails to add that Israel actively participated in the massacre of indigenous Africans by steadily supplying arms to the apartheid South African regime. At the time, Tel Aviv argued that the odious apartheid government was the former xerographic copy, because both nations were surrounded by hostile countries; in the case of Israel, it was the Arab world, while on the African continent it was the indigenes, whom both white South Africa and Israel considered to be unworthy of the franchise or democratic empowerment. Here in New York, for example, former mayor Edward I. Koch wrote reams of articles justifying the brazen complicity of the State of Israel with apartheid governmental brutalities on the rather bizarre, if also cynical, grounds that the racist regime was a great protector and friend of South African Jews. Now if this warped logic does not sound like a paragraph culled out of Hitler's *Mein Kampf*, what does? It may also be recalled that Mr. Koch made the preceding remark in the wake of Archbishop Desmond Tutu's acute and empirical observation, while visiting the State of Israel, that the Israeli government's ill-treatment of the Palestinians bore striking similarity with the erstwhile apartheid regime's maltreatment of Africans.

Mr. Bernstein also faults European critics of Israel, some of whom have called for the dissolution of the Jewish state, for being biased simply because ardent and prominent critics such as A.N. Wilson and Jose Saramago, a Portuguese Nobel Literature laureate, have not also called for the dissolution of Rwanda and the Congo, where hundreds of thousands have died as a result of "intertribal slaughter." Indeed, the fact that, unlike Israel, Rwanda and Congo are not settler colonies is a point that seems to be too insufferable for Mr. Bernstein to acknowledge. And what is more, as repellent as the Rwandan-Burundian-Congolese genocide may be, elementary historical knowledge points to their slavo-colonial mintage. And to be sure, it was the determined and concerted efforts of ardent pan-Africanists like Ghana's Kwame Nkrumah and Congo's Patrice Lumumba at resolving this continental contretemps and seemingly intractable riddle that induced the wanton wrath of Washington via its Central Intelligence Agency (CIA).

It is also interesting to recall that run underneath Mr. Bernstein's article were three photographs of the Rwandan genocide. To the left-hand corner of a grim picture showcasing exhumed skeletal remains of Rwandan victims of the 1994 massacre was annotated: "The war put a sudden, brutal end to a shortlived period of great optimism about Africa." This most blisteringly presumptuous, if also unpardonably ignorant, remark was credited to Norimitsu Onishi, *The New York Times'* leading correspondent on African affairs. To begin with, neither Rwanda nor the Congo constitutes the collective destiny of the African continent, a geopolitical landmass which is about four times the size of the United States. And, also, while these two countries have undoubtedly great economic potentialities, the major beneficiaries over the past 300 years, conservatively speaking, have almost wholly been the West, not the rest of the African continent. Furthermore, less than ten percent of Africans live in this so-called Heart-of-Darkness. This, of course, is not to imply that the fortunes (and misfortunes) of Rwanda and Congo are not integral to the fortunes (and misfortunes) of the entire continental African populace; it is simply to caution critics against the racist misrepresentation of the continent by its weakest links. Indeed, one would not project the destiny of the entire European community on the basis of the recent political histories of the former Yugoslavia and Ireland.

One of the brazen pretexts by which Washington and the West have condoned Israeli atrocities against the Palestinians has been to disingenuously tout Israel as the only genuine democracy in the Middle-East. Needless to say, apartheid South Africa under F.W. deKlerk and his predecessors was also democratic. The fascist attempt by *The New York Times* to vindicate Israeli atrocities against Palestinians by poor-mouthing Africans would not wash; Africans are too intelligent for this kind of slavo-colonial poppycock, and so is most of the rest of the world.

Ultimately, the contingency of an African renaissance cannot be predicated solely upon the checkered fortunes of Rwanda and Congo. Such a salutary resurgence would involve the entire continent, and when that happens, particularly in the wake of a continental African Union, a la ideological Nkrumah-ism, it would be Africans themselves, not the editors and reporters of *The New York Times*, who would announce it to the world.

17

Choosing Between Dignity and Famine

The New York Times' article was headlined "Between Famine and Politics, Zambians Starve." It was bylined Henri E. Cauvin and datelined Lusaka, Zambia, August 29, 2002. Of course, as has become commonplace with mainstream America's putative newspaper of record, the truth lay somewhere between the title and what was omitted from the content of the story. And what was omitted was the fact that Africa has had a long relationship with the United States, perhaps much longer than with any other continent or country but Britain, based on wanton unilateral dehumanization, abject exploitation and outright marginalization, which even in the best of times verges on what W.E.B. DuBois might have poignantly characterized as one of "amused contempt."

The aforementioned article suggested that out of her ineffable magnanimity, the United States government, sensing the extreme danger of famine in the southern African sub-region, had dispatched hundreds of metric tons of food which, curiously, some of the hardest hit African countries refused to accept. The preceding seemed to sharply contradict the age-old dictum that: "A beggar has no choice." To the average Western mindset, such attitude grossly contravened the time-tested bounds of empirical logic. Interestingly, however, as with many other cases in the past, there is a critical history behind this quizzical African reaction which most of the largely complacent Aryan world has not been wont to accepting. It is the history of unvarnished bad-faith.

In 1978 in Ghana, for example, while this writer was in secondary school, and there occurred a severe nationwide drought, good old Uncle Sam shipped in hundreds of tons of yellow-corn to enable his countryfolk brace up for the impending famine. To be certain, some palpable sort of famine had already palled the land by the eve of Uncle Sam's largesse. Nevertheless, Ghanaians would shortly regret having asked our benevolent "mother's brother" for food aid at all. For it would soon be determined that the yellow-corn largesse was a vintage Trojan horse, as many who had consumed the maize, both in the form of grits and seed, came down with acute cases of diarrhea. This alarming situation prompted some Ghanaian scientists to run laboratory tests on samples of Uncle Sam's food, only to discover to our horror that the yellow-corn was actually a fattened variety meant for livestock—animal feed, to be more precise and scientific.

In the case of Zambia, and the other southern African states, the problem is one of genetically engineered corn. No matter, because we are also given to understand that this variety of corn tends "to be more resistant to worms," and such other vermin; and also that it is "now widely consumed in the United States." For Zambians, however, the problem is one of cross-pollination and the woeful possibility of contaminating the non-engineered (or organic) local food supply. This concern is quite significant, being that a "number of scientists and consumer advocates argue [that] the effects of genetic engineering on both the environment and consumers have not been adequately examined" (*Times* 8/30/02:A6). And who can reasonably dispute the fact that Africa and Africans are too ecologically fragile to be subjected to the dicey game of corporate biotechnology?

The preceding maugre, mulling the **New York Times** report, one gets the rather visceral, if also primitivistic impression that for a hungry person all that matters is simply getting some food to eat. With this kind of logic, to question the comestibility of charitable food amounts to sheer lunacy. Forget about the fact that here, in the United States, hundreds of successful lawsuits are launched or filed by consumers against food-processing companies every year, aimed at guaranteeing both the unfettered enjoyment of food and the preservation of public health. Which is why it is quite interesting to note that accompanying the *Times*' story is the high-definition photograph of a Zambian woman picking kernels of food from a macadamized highway, with the rather cynical and outrightly insulting caption: Zambians now scavenge for food. [Ms] Aluniya Ngulube picked kernels of [genetically engineered?] corn spilled off a truck last week"

In the Ghanaian case, narrated at the beginning of this article, the coordinator for Uncle Sam's largesse was Mr. Craig Schuler, a then-Peace Corps teacher at St. Peter's Secondary School, Nkwatia-Kwahu, where the writer was a student. Mr. Schuler hailed from one of the mid-western states—Ohio or Iowa?—so it was quite appropriate that he anchor his country's food-distribution network in Ghana from the port at Takoradi. But whether Mr. Schuler truly believed that he was about the sacred and respectable business of feeding God's hungry and poor, remains quite another discursive subject for the future.

We are also, significantly, apprised of the fact that Zambia and some of the other southern African states trade considerably with countries of the European Union, "which requires all genetically modified products to be so labeled." Thus to avoid being totally shut out of the international market, it becomes imperative for technologically underdeveloped African countries to studiously guard against the veritable threat of genetically engineered food. The collective destiny of the continent is, therefore, what is at stake. Interestingly, America, a country renowned for its unparalleled leadership foresight on issues of health and commerce, looks at Africans emulating her sterling example and imperiously exclaims, "How dare you!" instead of applauding the bold and courageous efforts of these putative "special education students."

Indeed, there is a short passage in Chinua Achebe's classic novel **Things Fall Apart** (1958), I suppose, in which a lizard that inadvertently falls off a tree says proudly to himself: "If no-one would praise me, then I shall praise myself."

18

Baghdad—The New Japan

In the wake of the World Trade Center, Pentagon and Pennsylvania attacks by elements with suspected links to Al Qaeda and the erstwhile Taliban government of Afghanistan, this writer grimly observed at a faculty meeting in his department at Nassau Community College that the United States was precariously perched on the brink of proto-colonial imperialism. This conclusion was reached mainly on the basis of the fact that up to the moment of the carpet-bombing of Afghanistan, and its oblique occupation by American and British forces, as well as the forces of a few other allied nations, our government had made no serious attempt at explaining to us how Osama Bin Laden, a man the Reagan-Bush administration had reportedly staunchly backed during the Soviet occupation of Afghanistan, would suddenly train turrets on Washington in the protean name of Jihad, or an Islamic Holy War. The country needed an explanation not simply because we, particularly those of us ardent students and keen observers of United States foreign policy, lacked a remarkable appreciation of the grim implications of the attacks, but more because ours was a government by consensus. Unfortunately, all that we were hearing was how some people and some countries, particularly among those of Islamic persuasion, were incorrigibly dead-set against the interests, aspirations and the very existence of the United States.

Indeed, the preceding posture brazenly ignored the time-tested law of Nature, which logically posits the inextricable inter-linkage between action and reaction. This simply means that even the seemingly gratuitous, antisocial acts of the legally insane have been known to have their roots in the very dynamics of nature and nurture, as it were. And this was why I exhorted my colleagues to assume the imperative moral stance dictated by their self-chosen profession—assuming, in fact, that they were no mere hirelings—to explain some of the salient factors behind the infamous September 11 assaults to their students. Among the Akan-speaking people of Ghana, this writer intimated, was a proverb which noted that: "When one disregards the civic rules of human conduct by keeping company with hounds, one is almost certain to have one's lips licked by the unsavory." For some, the obvious may not be envisaged as such, being that we live in a relativistic society.

That Washington seems hell-bent on a proto-colonial course of action, one that is ineluctably inimical to our long-term interests, became evident in an article which appeared in the Online edition of *The New York Times* of October 11, 2002. The article alleged that: "The White House [was] developing a detailed plan modeled on the postwar occupation of Japan, to install an American-led military government in Iraq if the United States topple[d] Saddam Hussein." The article attributed the preceding quote, an obviously deliberate press leak, to some anonymous "senior administration officials." All along, we thought that we had been ushered into Twenty-First Century Post-Colonial Governance—at least that is how most of the literature of the non-Western world is labeled at academic and cultural conferences nowadays. Perhaps some "senior administration officials" would do us great service by reminding the rest of the world that on the political calendar of the United States "real colonialism" is just beginning. If so, then Ghana's Kwame Nkrumah was grossly mistaken in the late 1950s when the astute political thinker coined the term "neocolonialism" to designate a sophisticated rule by corporeal proxy, albeit ideological clones, in the historical epoch of triumphal independence movements. But whether 40 years after the fact, any country would be so pliable as to exhibit such intellectual obtuseness as to render a proto-colonial regime a practical reality as the Bush II administration seems to envisage for Baghdad, remains to be seen.

But that the success of proto-colonialism depends largely on a critical mass of fifth-columnists or quislings is apparent from the fact that, according to *The New York Times* report, our country's strongman intends to govern the "Iraqis, perhaps, through a consultative council, [which] would assist an American-led military and, later, a civilian administration...[and that it is] Only after this transition would the American-led government hand power to Iraqis." Indeed, if the preceding reeks of all that is fatuous and risible, it is largely because it puts Washington in the unsavory seat of Divine Kingship, the very repugnant position for which the extant British monarch suffered untold and ringing humiliation in the historic emanation of the august American Revolution in the late eighteenth century. Or is it simply because the insuperable trait of humanity is to keep repeating past mistakes?

Indeed, the mercurial if also quite questionable, Dr. Henry A. Kissinger put it best when the former U.S. Secretary of State recently asserted that he was "viscerally opposed to [any] prolonged occupation of a Muslim country at [sic] the heart of the Muslim world by Western nations who [have arrogated to themselves] the right to re-educate that country." And, needless to say, Dr. Kissinger should know better about these things than most of us, having himself served as a district administrator in the American military-occupied Germany of the post-World War II era. Then again, as a colleague intimated to this writer in the wake of the September 11 catastrophe, "When one is not an elected leader, how can one be expected to amply appreciate the finer points of justice and democracy as one staple ideological diet?"

The New York Times article titled "U.S. Has a Plan to Occupy Iraq, Officials Report," and bylined David E. Sanger and Eric Schmitt, observes that a U.S. occupation of Iraq would be the sort of economic bonanza that Afghanistan has not been. For starters, "It would put an American officer in charge of Iraq for a year or more while the United States and its allies searched for weapons and maintained Iraq's oil fields. For as long as the coalition partners administered Iraq, they would essentially control the second largest proven reserves of oil in the world, nearly 11 percent of the total. A senior official said [that] the United Nations' oil-for-food program would be expanded to help finance stabilization and reconstruction."

Essentially, the preceding is a crudely borrowed page from the odious tome of British colonial imperialism, whereby the natural and human resources of the colonized are unevenly siphoned to underwrite the economic development of the colonizer and other less profitable colonies, with a piddling modicum of such surplus going into the cosmetic development of the primarily exploited, as happened to Ghana (the erstwhile Gold Coast) during London's imperial domination of the so-called British West Africa. Already, we see the Iraqi opposition which, by the way, seems quite happy to come along for a ride on a bus whose destination is anywhere but Baghdad; and then we have Mr. Zalmay Khalilzad, the special assistant to Mr. Bush II for Near-Eastern, Southwest Asian and North African affairs. Indeed, Mr. Khalilzad, whose Arabo-Islamic provenance can be nominally inferred, suggested in a recent public presentation that "The coalition [of Western imperialist nations] will assume…responsibility for the territorial defense and security of Iraq after liberation." Perhaps somebody had better plead with the Arab League to dispatch an emergency posse of dyed-in-the-wool stratocrats into Washington to save us from the Bush II "constitutional" monarchy.

19

Media Terrorism in Ghana

An August 1, 2002, story posted on the Internet reported the issuance of two anonymous death threats against Mr. Kweku Baako, editor of the privately-owned newspaper *The Crusading Guide*. The threats were in response to the allegedly persistent attacks by Mr. Baako on former President Jerry John Rawlings and his wife, Nana Konadu Agyemang-Rawlings. As far as those of us among the inky fraternity are concerned, there is nothing fundamentally remiss with *The Crusading Guide*'s editor's apparently unmitigable and relentless attempts at exposing the purported "expensive lifestyles of the Rawlingses, who over 20 years ago, considered rich people in the society as criminals who did not deserve to live" (*newsinghana.com* 8/1/02). Indeed, such glaring evidence as the brazen expropriation of the businesses of Ghanaian entrepreneurs like Mr. Siaw, of Tata Brewery, are all too raw in our memory for anybody to pretend that in seeking to rekindle our sense of "probity and accountability," the editor of *The Crusading Guide* may be unduly harassing the Rawlingses.

What further testifies to the need to putting the Ghanaian public on high, perpetual alert is the fact that until a Supreme Court order proscribed his treasonous activities very recently, Mr. Rawlings and his cohorts insisted on celebrating the hitherto unilaterally institutionalized anniversary of the so-called June 4th Revolution. The latter, to-date, remains the most untenable sanguinary pretext in the country's political history. Under the specious guise of a "house-cleaning exercise," Mr. Rawlings supervised the systematic liquidation of his perceived personal enemies, who were also summarily branded as enemies of the revolution and thus the nation at large. This was also the period that witnessed the well-orchestrated destruction of the salutary development of home-grown capitalist. Our protagonist would later issue a disingenuous and half-hearted parliamentary apology for "mistakes" committed during the infamous AFRC-PNDC eras. It is, however, quite amusing to recognize the fact that Mr. Rawlings actually presumes his unilateral and rather cavalier apology to have been unreservedly accepted by his countrymen and women.

Furthermore, this firebrand champion of pseudo-socialism has almost overnight converted himself into an ardent believer in the very market economy that he single-handedly destroyed in the country. It is this paradoxical state of affairs which seems to inform much of what Mr. Kweku Baako, Jr., and his newspaper purvey in terms of the national discourse on political probity. The only people who could sincerely go against this brand of journalism are obviously those who benefited from the extortionate reign of terror unleashed on Ghanaians by the governments of the so-called Provisional National Defense Council and the National Democratic Congress. The preceding praxis is called "development journalism." It is extensively practiced throughout the world, particularly in the so-called Third World countries where the indispensable centrality of the mass media to socioeconomic, cultural and political development cannot be overemphasized. Where the media are allowed by governments to pursue an independent policy of informational primacy, as opposed to merely serving as passive conduits of official agendas, the end-result is one of collective national cognitive acuity. Under the Rawlings administration, however, the contrary or the counterproductive ideology of "His Master's Voice" came to characterize the Ghanaian media landscape. One either fatuously sang paeans to officialdom, regardless of the climate or the level and tenor of its performance, or one shortly found oneself occupationally proscribed and personally endangered. There are amply documented cases where the (P)NDC government caused the arrest and immurement of journalists accused of deliberately maligning the former merely because the latter had sought to bridge an artificially created information gap by publishing the unofficial versions of what they perceived and believed to constitute the ontic goings-on in The Castle—the Ghanaian coordinate of the White House.

While Mr. Kweku Baako, Jr., is squarely within his rights to call the game as he sees it, nevertheless, the fiery pen-pusher's rather intemperate declaration on a radio program, to the effect, that he intended to "strip [Mr.] Rawlings naked" to the bones, amounted to fighting words. The crusading editor ought to have finetuned his rhetoric without temporizing his ideological focus on development-oriented journalism. The issue is not a raw case of simply humiliating Mr. Rawlings, it is, more importantly, pointing out the inescapable hypocrisy that invariably subtends the lives of self-appointed monarchs and executioners.

For its part the substantive, or ruling, government need to issue a strong warning against those who seek to undermine healthy public discourse, the very foundation of any modern civilized society. A prison sentence of, for instance, five years for anybody caught in the dastardly act of having issued an anonymous threat against the life of any journalist would, definitely, be a positive initiative. Needless to say, the institution of journalism underpins the very human act of critical thinking and literacy development. These disciplinary areas are in dire demand in post-NDC Ghana. Any attempt, therefore, to undermine these fundamental elements of constructive public discourse, indisputably amounts to the summary destruction of our very humanity. The government must not wait until these dastardly threats are consummated before bringing the culprits to book; for, as the adage goes: "To be forewarned is to be forearmed."

20

The Problem of Exam Leakage

It has often been argued that the greatest challenge to African development is the dearth or acute lack of foreign exchange and foreign investment. And while the significant realities of the preceding cannot be gainsaid, the peremptory fact of national self-investment is invariably and woefully ignored. It is almost as if foreign investment in itself, short of public and administrative accountability, is all that there is to our collective socioeconomic, political and cultural development.

It is with the foregoing squarely in view that the recent summary cancellation in Ghana of this year's [i.e. 2000's] Basic Education Certificate Examinations (BECE), formerly called General Certificate of Education (GCE), by the country's Ministry of Education (Newsinghana.com—May 18, 2002) must be deemed as a grievous breach of public trust and accountability. That the untoward phenomenon of examination leakage seems to have become a perennial event, almost like an annual festal celebration, is rather bizarre and embarrassing. It is almost as if the Ghanaian leadership cannot be trusted with the preservation of our nation's academic and cultural integrity. What makes the situation even more damning is the fact that until very recently the Ghanaian educational system ranked as the best on the entire African continent.

This writer takes the problem of examination leakage very seriously and personally, having lost two long years of his academic career by paying for the reckless negligence of educational authorities. Needless to say, the blanket annulment of examinations suspected to have been leaked, while it conveys a theoretical sense of justice is, of course, grossly unjust, particularly with regard to diligent students located in the rural areas of the country. Invariably incidents of leakage have tended to be primarily concentrated in the urban areas, viz.: Accra, Kumasi, Koforidua, Cape Coast, Sekondi-Takoradi, Sunyani, Tamale, Ho, Tema, Wa, Bolgatanga, among a host of other municipalities. The Internet revolution notwithstanding—and it is interesting to note that most library cataloging in Ghana's leading universities continues to be done manually—examination leakage is an urban sub-cultural anomaly. For instance, during the five years that this writer attended St. Peter's Secondary School, at Kwahu-Nkwatia, in the Eastern Region of Ghana, between the mid-1970s and early 1980s, he never set eyes on, let alone get hold of, a copy of leaked examination papers. Indeed, it was not until he transferred to Kumasi, the unofficial Ghanaian cultural capital, to attend the world-renowned Prempeh College, that he stumbled across a **genuine** leaked examination paper. Needless to say, so morally devastating, traumatic and blistering was the experience that this writer, dazed with utter disbelief, almost failed his own exam!

It was also in Kumasi that I came to appreciate the damnable fact that examination leakage had a culture all its own. To be certain, it was a going concern, with some veteran teachers and headmasters widely rumored to be deeply involved, particularly some of the senior teachers who served as examiners for the West African Examinations Council (WAEC). The grapevine also held that these teachers leaked examination questions and papers in order to ingratiate themselves with their often under-prepared and examination-shy students, who then came to regard the former as demi-gods and prophets. Indeed, there was an incident in May 1982, when some students of Prempeh College and Yaa Asantewaa Secondary School, both located in Kumasi, were rounded up and detained overnight for interrogation by law-enforcement agents. My elder cousin, who is now a chief inspector of police, then a detective corporal, handled the case. And although it was forensically established that the players involved had purchased leaked exam papers, nothing came of the matter. This was partly because Prempeh College was attended by the sons and wards of the wealthy and powerful in Ghanaian society. Indeed, at the time, a top executive of WAEC was a Prempeh College alumnus.

The summary and blanket cancellation of national examinations, as a result of purportedly massive leakage, carries in its trail at least two deleterious psychological ramifications. First of all, it inevitably dampens the spirits of otherwise diligent and honest students; and this has a long-term impact on national development. For some of these students become unmitigably cynical about the credibility of standardized examinations, and may eventually drop out of school altogether. Secondly, such policy move damages the credibility and integrity of the national educational system, both internally and externally. Of course, the third factor is that those who are able to get away with exam cheating eventually do succeed to responsible academic, corporate and professional positions for which they are obviously not qualified, thereby perpetuating the proverbial vicious cycle of intellectual and professional dishonesty.

As of this writing[June 2002], the top-brass of Ghana's education ministry, led by Professor Christopher Ameyaw-Ekumfi, a cabinet carry-over from the Rawlings administration, claims to have effected the arrest of some of the culprits involved in the leakage. Unfortunately, however, those who have been arrested so far consist largely of printers, messengers and other low-level personnel. Needless to say, what ought to happen for this perennial contretemps to be remedied once-and-for-all, is for the government to recall or immediately dismiss the entire membership of the top echelons of Ghana's Ministry of Education, as would almost certainly be done here in the United States under similar circumstances. The top constabulary of the Ministry of Education cannot claim to have been unaware of the leakage problem; should they claim innocence or ignorance, that would be all the more reason to effect their immediate removal—for this is a veritable indication of administrators being woefully and unpardonably out of touch with their portfolios. And for good measure, parliament and the judiciary should also pave the way for aggrieved students and parents to initiate lawsuits against the Ministry of Education and the government, in general, for their gross dereliction of duty.

Forcing students to re-sit examinations at the expense of the Ministry of Education, and thus at the ultimate expense of the Ghanaian public at large, as Minister Ameyaw-Ekumfi has blandly enjoined, is no salutary remedy. At best, it amounts to a sheer waste of scarce budgetary resources. Somebody must be made to pay for the humongous cost involved in forcing students to re-sit their exams; garnishing the salaries of top personnel of WAEC and the Ministry of Education may well be a lesson quite worthy of emulation. The neocolonial, plantation-approach to discipline has outlived its usefulness in the twenty-first century.

21

American Taliban

"Now tell me, Professor, you don't really think [that] John Walker Lindh is like Mandela, do you?" That was 25-year-old Eric Healy, a technical military service-man and summer school student in my "Early American Literature" course. The course is a comprehensive survey of both oral and chirographical literature dating from the pre-colonial era up to the wake of the landmark Revolutionary era. In the aftermath of September 11 [2001], I have attempted to link the latter catas-trophe to the protracted and perennial catastrophe that epitomized the brutal conquest and Euro-people of the so-called New World. The overriding theme has been the label of "Terrorism," its wide-ranging rhetorical ramifications, and the fact that such pontifical grandstanding, largely on the part of our major polit-ical figures, as witnessed in the immediate aftermath of September 11, smacks of the unmitigably and unpardonably hypocritical and outrightly nonsensical. Of course, in the preceding, the perspectives adopted are diasporic African and indigenous American (I refuse to accept the anachronistic appropriation of the term Native-American; American Indian is also one which I consider to be rather ideologically and culturally perverse).

"Now tell me, Professor, you don't really think [that] John Walker Lindh is like Mandela, do you?"

Of course, I consider John Walker Lindh to be a veritable American Mandela. And this assertion should in no way be deemed to be evocative of the purely dis-cursive concept of "Devil's Advocate"; I consider neither our subject nor any offi-cially designated "Enemy-of-State" in recent American history as such. To be certain, it is these quick-to-label-others breed of neo-conservative Republican Party chief constables who, in practical terms, fit the description of statal or national enemies. And I, also, believe that the United States' Constitution obliges me—as well as other conscientious writers and scholars—to play the critical and indispensable role of honest and constructive citizenship in no uncertain terms.

98

This also implies that I, like all Americans, reserve the right to responsible and transparent leadership.

Indeed, whether you call him "Johnny Jihad," as the New York *Daily News* (7/16/02) did, or "American Taliban," as *New York Post*'s Andrea Peyser self-righteously declared in her rather desultory column of July 16 [2001], the interesting story of John Walker Lindh is also the story of our collective ideological and moral integrity, or the lack thereof. And the latter two essential elements of human civilization are what, I firmly believe, we sorely lack as a polity. For instance, Ms. Peyser, in her rather starry-eyed, to say little of cognitively dissonant, column priggishly sneers: "Taliban Johnny's dad was on the radio yesterday. And the California loony who bred a true American turncoat was comparing his boy to a world-famous former prisoner: Nelson Mandela."

What is both intriguing and puzzling about the preceding quote is its paradoxical truthfulness. Indeed unless one possesses the memory bank of a chicken, one cannot be seriously outraged by the preceding, seemingly anomalous comparison. Those of us who have lived long enough to remember the grim Apartheid years know that for some three decades, Nelson R. Mandela, Govan Mbeki, Oliver Tambo, Walter Sissulu, Winnie Mandela and the rest of the African National Congress (ANC) constabulary were known and labeled "terrorists" by Washington and the rest of the Western world, the so-called international community. Indeed, on the eve of Mandela's kangaroo trial and life-term sentence and imprisonment, the United States government read the same ideological page as Pretoria; and throughout the former South African president's 27-and-half years in Robben Island's maximum security prison, both Mandela and other members of the ANC, as well as other democracy-loving anti-apartheid activists, were being variably designated "communists," "rebels," "rascals" and outright nincompoops. And so it is quite amusing for mainstream pen-pushers like Andrea Peyser to summarily assay an abrogation of our collective historical memory, simply because it has become rather routine and pedestrian to call the proverbial cat a bad name in order to facilitate its speedy execution.

And talking of execution, this is what the seemingly, utterly frustrated Ms. Peyser writes on her subject of vile and vitriol: "It may sound twisted to you and me to hear Lindh's daddy compare his boy to Nelson Mandela—jailed 27 years for resisting South Africa's apartheid regime. But he is on to something./Just watch. Over the next two decades, through interview, biography and fan club, Lindh will transform [himself] from traitor to martyr—a victim of the big, bad American system. Then, still in his prime, he'll be free./He should have been executed for treason."

Needless to say, 38 years ago, many Westerners of Andrea Peyser's ideological bent or suasion cried for the blood of Nelson Mandela. And to be certain, the only reason why the now-globally celebrated Mandela has lived to this day is because at the time of the infamous Rivonia Trial, the South African judicial system did not have a death-penalty clause for such vintage political prisoners. It is significant and interesting to add, however, that such judicial lack did not prevent the white apartheid regime from summarily executing the likes of Bantu Stephen Biko. Furthermore, those of us who had the great misfortune living through the Reaganomic era of Constructive Engagement find the likes of such dishonest, misguided and fanatical (and right-wing) ideologues as Ms. Peyser to be far more dangerous than the myriad Walker Lindhs of this world. To date, Washington has yet to apologize for her willful and disgraceful complicity in orchestrating the familial destruction of the Mandelas, among a host of others.

In the final analysis, the question becomes not one of whether anybody believes that John Walker Lindh is the American political rejoinder or ideological coordinate of Nelson Mandela's. Rather, it borders on whether a capricious misalignment of political paradigms warrants our self-righteous, if also outright hypocritical, outrage.

22

Ekwueme Presidency: A Moral Contradiction

The article began pontifically with an obstreperous neocolonialist zeal: "Dr. Alex I. Ekwueme is probably the most [best?] educated and one of the most experienced, true politicians on the continent of Africa. No one who knows this giant of [a] man would doubt that his political pedigree is the real deal. An immensely successful American-trained architect, lawyer, businessman, British Ph.D., and a great philanthropist, Dr. Ekwueme is a man that intrigues and appeals [sic]. He was the Vice President of Nigeria under the presidency of Alhaji Shehu Usman Aliyu Shagari, 1979–1983, before the military truncated the Second Republic, which Obasanjo's military regime had installed" (*African Market News*, April 2002).

That the preceding quote appeared as part of a front-cover feature, almost editorial-like, was less embarrassing than its damning implication that two generations after political self-governance, the erstwhile British colonial subject continued to evaluate his or her societal worth and personal integrity under a Eurocentric cultural rubric. Needless to say, to wholly predicate one's educational attainment, and thus one's cultural refinement, on purely academic grounds gives withering, if also morally sobering, short-shrift to the very concept of education. And what is even more disconcerting is the fact that the curriculum on which such measurement is based has African values, socioeconomic and cultural needs squarely located on its margins. And if, indeed, a "British Ph.D." or, for that matter, even its coordinate American breed, meant anything beyond an academic transcript, needless to say, most of Anglophone Africa would not be in the sorry state of affairs in which we currently find ourselves.

To be certain, what gives any level of academic credential its worth in designation is the demonstrable instrumentality of the holder to the general development and betterment of society. In the preceding sphere, Dr. Alex Ekwueme is not without his laurels; however, it is also significant to recall that his credential as "Vice-" President to Mr. Shehu Shagari could not be patently affirmed as one of sterling depth and breadth. For, wasn't it under President Shagari that the "legendary" Mr. Dikko (allegedly a brother-in-law to Dr. Ekwueme) reportedly squirreled over $100million of Nigeria's hard-earned foreign exchange into the bloated and parasitic vaults of European banks? And unless all of us are afflicted with sound-bite memory banks, then perhaps one could aptly conclude that the "vice-"president of a veritable "Thuggocracy," as that which Nigeria witnessed under Alhaji Shehu Shagari, with its untold state of wanton wastage, hardly deserves a second chance at national stewardship.

Let no one be fooled, unalloyed personal achievements do not automatically translate into public service success stories. In the former circumstance, there is a vested interest, one's very livelihood and economic well-being are at stake, whereas in the latter situation such interest, at best, is vicarious and relatively remote. And this is why, for instance, corporate proprietors who would ordinarily not brook the least hint or manifestation of managerial negligence or incompetence, oftentimes seem to possess highly elastic tolerance capacity for public malfeasance. This, indeed, is the one solid instance in which the adage of charity beginning at home woefully falls short of the norm. It is, therefore, rather sad that Dr. Ekwueme's purportedly unimpeachable personal integrity did not appreciably contribute to the critical stanching of administrative venality or misprision during the infamous Shagari era.

Then we are also deafeningly apprised of the fact that Dr. Ekwueme was such an irreproachable "party loyalist [that the former "vice-"president] supported the military-propelled candidacy of retired General Matthew Okikiola Aremu Olusegun Obasanjo (OBJ)." If the preceding behavioral aberration, on the part of Dr. Ekwueme, is to be lauded, as one presumes *African Market News* publisher Felix Agidigbi to be implying, then Nigerians may be in for great trouble should Dr. Ekwueme assay a presidential run and actually win. For, needless to say, "a party loyalist [who] supports a military-propelled [presidential] candidate" is no well-meaning patriot; at best, this breed of politician is a brazen opportunist.

The author of the above-referenced article also seems to have fore-knighted or pre-ordained a sure-footed stable of unassailable political potentates for national leadership in the foreseeable future, thus his rather cavalier inference: "With the presidency of President Obasanjo doing badly in keeping Nigeria equitably afloat, and especially with the recent ploy by politicians to keep [sic] their jobs by urging OBJ to contest in 2003, many people are wondering what it would take to draft Dr. Alexander Ifeanyichukwu Ekwueme to lead Nigeria out of another darkness enveloping the political landscape. The prospect of a President Ekwueme brightened recently with the withdrawal of retired General Ibrahim Badamosi Babangida (IBB) from contention. It is left for Obasanjo to do the right [thing]: Run! Yes, run back to his Ota Farms and play the role he does very well: Statesman."

Alas, it does not seem to this writer that the *African Market News* editorialist adequately appreciates the significance of being a statesman (or—woman, for that matter), as opposed to merely being a politician. Consequently, regarding his "anointed" candidate for the 2003 Nigerian presidential election, the author observes: "Dr. Ekwueme, on the other hand, is a consummate politician. He knows that all it would take to resolve certain issues is patient dialogue. He has the humility required to rule a complex country such as Nigeria."

Well, maybe so, but then our peremptory kingmaker also defines the contradictory terms of his own ideological objective thusly: "A soldier thinks more of the next war; a politician thinks more of winning the next election, while a statesman is more interested in the next generation." Needless to say, by the logic of his own argument, undoubtedly taken out of context from Dr. Biodun Onilude, of the University of Ibadan, our *African Market News* editorialist seems to suggest that President Obasanjo is the foremost Nigerian statesman, the one who "is more interested in the next generation." And who can dispute the fact that the presidency of any post-colonial polity is about the preservation of the stability of that polity's collective national destiny for the next generation?

23

Sharia and Sexism

An Islamic court in the northern Nigerian city of Funtua recently sentenced a 31-year-old woman to death by stoning for having a child out of wedlock. The sentence was supposedly in consonance with ***sharia*** or Islamic law. The woman, Amina Lawal Kurami, a divorcee, was reportedly granted a two-year reprieve while she nursed and weaned her baby-daughter.

What makes this case, originally reported by Reuters news agency, interesting is that it is suggestive of the proverbial "Immaculate Conception," the very unscientific notion that short of cloning and artificial insemination, a woman could conceive and bear a normal human child without coitus or sexual intercourse with a man. Interestingly, however, Ms. Kurami was not charged with self-sexualization, which means that she had apparently engaged in sexual activity with a man in order to become pregnant and bring forth her daughter. The simple, intelligent question thus becomes: "If it is, indeed, against Islamic law to have a child outside of marriage, should not both couple involved in this act of 'sacrilege' by equally punished?" The fact that Islamic culture, generally speaking, accords a relatively minimal or negligible degree of power to women vis-à-vis their menfolk should logically render these men more culpable for untoward social expression of adult sexuality than their women. This is because it is highly unlikely that Amina Lawal Kurami coerced any man to engage her in sexual intercourse. It is also almost certain that the man with whom she had sex, and by whom she bore her child was privy to the Koranic edict prohibiting having children out of wedlock. It also goes without saying that the man who engaged Ms. Kurami in extra-marital congress knew that such act was more likely than not to lead to pregnancy and childbirth.

Needless to say, the very process by which the court arrived at its verdict is, to say the least, flagrantly suspect. First of all, we are told that not a single woman sat among the bench of five judges who delivered the verdict. This, of course, means that the perspectives of women on the crucial issue of adultery, a crime for which they solely stand to be meted the death penalty, was either not seriously considered or was simply ignored. And by proscribing the jural input and perspectives of women automatically invalidates the verdict.

We are also not apprised of the exact details of the process by which incriminating evidence against the accused, now a convict, was elicited, except the rather glib fact that: "The judges based their decision mainly on what they said was a confession to adultery by [Ms.] Kurami…in [a] lower court trial" earlier on. And so we are left wondering whether, perhaps, Ms.Kurami's vengeful former husband colluded with this patently Kangaroo-like Islamic court to teach this apparently strong-willed and unflappably independent woman an indelible and fatal lesson. It is also interesting that these supposedly "religious judges" are so willing to speedily execute the mother of a toddler for the very "crime" whose product the latter delightfully is. "Delightfully" because no life is fundamentally less significant than another, regardless of gender or creed. In sum, the Kurami verdict tells us more about the pathologically primitive mindset of the judges than the purported anti-social behavior of the culprit. But perhaps even more importantly, we need to remind these patent ***Shariamaniacs*** that we are living in post-colonial Africa at the turn of the twenty-first century, not medieval Mecca or Katsina.

The pathological and pathetic ***Sharianization*** of northern Nigeria should raise serious concerns in the entire West African sub-region, particularly coming at a time when the latter's geopolitical landscape is fast becoming an organic unit. Indeed, just as the European Union put forth constructive and progressive civic stipulations as indispensable prerequisites to Turkey's admission into that august body of "civilized" nations, a similar stipulation must be encoded and rigidly enforced by the Economic Community of West African States (ECOWAS). The Nigerian government thus ought to take a strong and uncompromising leadership stance on this issue. So far, all that President Olusegun Obasanjo has done is make tentative and incoherent remarks about the possibility of his country risking international isolation on this question. Instead, the Obasanjo government and the Nigerian senate should move expeditiously to replace the glaringly anachronistic Islamic jural system with a secular, more modern and non-sexist alternative.

That this is not the first judicial travesty of its kind, must make the need to promptly revamp the ***Sharia*** system, or possibly scrap it altogether, imperative. In March this year [2002], for instance, another woman, Safiya Hussaini Tungar-Tudu, was sentenced to death by stoning. That sentence was reversed only after the European Union led a global appeal for clemency (Reuters 8/19/02). That it took Africa's former colonial masters to bring sanity to bear on such jural anomaly is rather embarrassing, particularly coming some forty-two years after we sent these socioeconomic and cultural cormorants back home.

It is, however, quite heartening and edifying to learn that in the very vanguard of the struggle against such judicial barbarism are such astute modern Muslim lawyers as Aliyu Musa Yauri and Hauwa Ibrahim, among a plethora of others. While many of us continue to lament the fact that the infamous Biafran War was allowed to happen at all, it goes without saying that extirpating the current sexist murder which parades in the name of religion is a battle the entire African continent cannot afford to lose.

24

Obed Asamoah and the "Abongo" Boys

Recently, the opposition National Democratic Congress (NDC) of Ghana held a day-long seminar during which the party leadership launched a so-called social democratic agenda as its political philosophy. That the preceding agenda is being spearheaded by Dr. Obed Asamoah, the party's chairman, makes the issue risible to the point of the outright ludicrous.

Four years ago [retrospective from 2002] when Dr. Asamoah was Attorney-General and Minister for Justice, I visited Ghana on the occasion of my mother's funeral; I stayed in the country for four weeks and did not like one bit what the NDC constabulary seemed to be about. Back then, having been in power for nearly 16 years, the Rawlings-led government could not supply the Ghanaian capital of Accra with ample electricity—so bad was the situation that energy had to be regulated alternatively among the various sections of the city. This meant that owning a refrigerator in one's home was practically useless, since one could not obtain power supply for more than 48 hours at a time, except, of course, if one privately owned a power plant or electricity generator. Needless to say, this problem had festered because for as long as the NDC—I "affectionately" call them the National Decapitators' Congress (or *Atetenkorona*, or Headchoppers Congress)—had monopolized the reins of governance in a virtual one-party state, the Akosombo Dam, the country's main source of hydroelectricity, had fallen into abject disrepair. It is significant to note that at the time of its commissioning in the early 1960s, Akosombo was the largest and finest of its kind in the entire West African sub-region. It would later be surpassed by the Kainji Dam in Nigeria.

Four years ago, Dr. Obed Asamoah also had reportedly had his house-boy—some claim it was a policeman—arrested and charged with stealing millions of Ghanaian cedis and some unspecified amount of U.S. dollars from the quondam Justice Minister's bedroom. Questioned about the source of such humongous sum at a time that the national coffers were dripping red, the grizzled party hack claimed that the money belonged to the ruling NDC party. He also insisted on his right as then-party secretary to hold onto the money for safe-keeping—the fact that he was not the party's treasurer did not, in the least, seem to matter. Another prominent party hack and sometime Ghanaian ambassador to the United Nations, Professor Kofi Awoonor, also reportedly accused his house-boy of stealing about $30,000 from the renowned poet and novelist's home. It would, therefore, be quite interesting to learn further about what Dr. Obed Asamoah and his cohorts mean when they talk of pursuing "a social democratic agenda" as the NDC's bona fide "political philosophy" (*newsinghana.com* 7/20/02).

Needless to say, while the performance of the ruling New Patriotic Party (NPP), led by the rhetorically languid if also stentorian President John Agyekum-Kufuor, has been anything but sterling, it is rather amusing to hear Dr. Asamoah characterize the NPP in the following terms: "If you see the drift, confusion, incompetence, ineptitude of the NPP government, you will appreciate the consequences of seeking power without adequately preparing for it" (*newsinghana.com* 7/20/02). Indeed, if the NDC top-dog sounds like a disgruntled British colonial governor on the eve of Ghana's independence to you, he may indeed be a neocolonialist avatar. For during the 20 years that the NDC held power, the party systematically undermined every vital institutional apparatus that makes for the salutary development of a modern civilized society.

Consequently, when NDC General-Secretary Dr. Josiah Aryeh says that his party is committed to "ensuring free tuition at the public tertiary level of education…with emphasis on science and technology, subject to the availability of resources (*newsinghana.com* 7/20/02), you definitely sense that the Legon Law School lecturer is either experiencing a delightful wet-dream or, perhaps, he takes most of his fellow citizens for fools. For starters, the Rawlings administration firmly shuttered the country's leading institutions of higher learning for at least half the number of years that the NDC held onto power. Indeed, so precarious was the situation that the British Broadcasting Corporation (BBC) reported awhile back that Britain was seriously reconsidering the coordinate validity of academic degrees awarded by Ghanaian universities, because recent graduates from these institutions performed at sub-standard levels. Many foreign companies with subsidiaries in the country also complained that sizable numbers of recent university graduates were woefully under-prepared for the job-market.

In the area of health, the situation is even more precarious, with hospitals having become virtual morgues and cemeteries. In fact, there is a running joke in Ghana that these days when one hears the siren of an ambulance racing through the principal streets of Accra, most likely it is a dead body being conveyed to the mortuary. In effect, nothing seems to be functioning traditionally or normally. The steady under-funding of hospitals has also meant a massive exodus of health personnel to regions of the proverbial greener pastures. All the while, Mr. Rawlings and his Abongo Boys were busy building commando divisions of the Ghana Armed Forces, in order to ensure their perennial cling to power. Which is why when party secretary Josiah Arayeh declares sanctimoniously that: "We must address the resource hierarchy as much as possible to ensure an equitable distribution of wealth in a world in which geo-economics is rapidly replacing geopolitics" (*newsinghana.com* 7/20/02), one wonders where he was when the Obed Asamoahs and Awoonors were distributing our country's and their party's funds in their bedrooms.

Interestingly, the NDC chairman also decries the meticulous process by which the NPP government has been arraigning corrupt members of the former ruling party before judicial systems of accountability. Dr. Asamoah is reported to be warning, among other remarks, that: "if a tradition was set [such] that the home of a politician after leaving office was the BNI [Bureau of National Investigations] cell or prison, then many men [and women?] of integrity and talent would shun public office" (*newsinghana.com*). It is worthwhile to recall that the BNI was established by the NDC in place of the erstwhile Special Branch (SB) of the Ghana Police Force, because the then-PNDC revolutionaries convinced themselves that the SB was too bureaucratic and conservative to effectively perform the NDC's dirty work of summarily convicting and executing or sentencing diligent Ghanaian entrepreneurs to harsh prison and other punitive terms. Back then, the revolutionary watch-phrase was "Probity and Accountability." And while one does not counsel retribution or witch-hunting, allowing political scam artists to get away with flagrant crimes against humanity and their fellow citizens is surely not the kind of "social democracy" that we understand Dr. Asamoah and his Abongo Boys to be advocating.

Indeed, the best strategy for the NDC and the good of Ghana is for the former not to seriously entertain any weird thoughts of coming back to power in 2004, "whether the NPP likes it or not"—for if they do actually make good on their quest for a tyrannical reprise, the NDC Abongo Boys must rest assured that they would not like what they shall be facing.

25

Playing Hardball with Presidential Imagery

The November 22 [2002] edition of Chris Matthews' "Hardball" (MSNBC-TV) featured a swirling controversy over the publication of a photograph of President George W. Bush II in the ***Chicago Tribune***, deemed to be rather unflattering and outright embarrassing. The picture depicted an emergency meeting between United Nations secretary-general Kofi Annan and the American premier at the White House over the raging Iraqi question. Mr. Bush is shown gesturing what appears to be a thumbs-up, with the jolly visage of an elementary schoolboy relishing his victory, over what, "Hardball" did not elucidate. The meeting came on the heels of the recent electoral sweep of both houses of Congress by the ruling Republican Party, and so one presumes the latter to have been the focus of such presidential mirth. And to be certain, there is absolutely nothing remiss with a politician savoring a fortuitous triumph in front of media cameras. After all, isn't contemporary politics all about ***telegenic dramaturgy***?

Alas, the phrase ***telegenic dramaturgy*** seems to have generated the controversial swirl around the ***Chicago Tribune***. Needless to say, in a country whose very mores have come to be almost wholly predicated upon public image, to be envisaged in bad pictorial light, as it were, is virtually tantamount to outright assassination. And while Mr. Bush's minions and supporters are not calling this apparent contretemps an assassination, the stark implication of the latter cannot be gainsaid. This is also where the surprise lies: For if anything at all, the political triumph of President Bush over former Vice-President Albert Gore, has been widely attributed to the fact that the latter sports the gelid demeanor of a robot, while the former decks the debonair mien of a pubescent junior high school pupil who just tasted the subliminal experience of first love. And so far, Mr. Bush seems to be choreographically living every bit of the part.

In any case, what seems to irk Mr. Bush's supporters regarding his unflattering photograph with the United Nations secretary-general is that, as usual, Mr. Annan looks the more dignified and presidential. And, indeed, it is just as it ought to be—for the man is a Ghanaian of royal heritage and lineage, as myriad of his countrymen and women both at home and abroad are. He is also of Akan cultural extraction, which means that even long before he became the diplomatic and political superstar that he now is, Uncle Kofi Atta was enlightened in the courtly ways and manners of future leaders. Here in America, unfortunately, there is as yet no known school for the rigorous and sterling ***character training*** of future leaders. And, what is worse, Martha Stewart's recent problems with Wall Street, as well as Congressional fiduciary watchdogs, does not seem to be paving the way, fast enough, for the salutary establishment of such august institution anytime soon.

Needless to say, more than any other cultural ingredient, leadership is about ***character***, or what may be aptly termed ***noblesse oblige***, that rarefied sense of moral and material responsibility that envisages global harmony and socioeconomic, political and cultural security as an organic whole. In fact, this is what distinguishes the average, well-cultivated Akan-Ghanaian leader from the average contemporary Western potentate. And here also, it is significant to note that whereas Mr. Bush has been described by many American critics, including some of his own ideological bedmates as an average leader, Mr. Kofi Annan has been said to more closely approximate or even paragon the proverbial cream of the crop. In sum, the latter has unbested diplomatic finesse, panache and intellectual heft, deft and agility. And for someone who belongs to a racial group that has been summarily relegated to the opposite and short-end of the measuring tape of dignity, integrity and moral rectitude, it is quite unthinkable to expect these sterling qualities perfectly minted in his very personality. Indeed, this is what the entire controversy seems to be about; which is why Mike Barnicle, of the New York ***Daily News***, appearing on Chris Matthews' "Hardball," bitterly lamented the fact that in the ***Chicago Tribune***'s photograph, it is Mr. Annan who better responds to the noble designation of "President of the United States," while Mr. Bush merely acts the inglorious part of a court jester. Indeed, in the aforementioned photograph, the distinguished Ghanaian chieftain looks more than presidential, with his gracefully relaxed posture, legs deftly crossed and fingers daintily clasped, and sitting straight and solemn, with a great thinker's rapt attention to his audience. Mr. Bush, on the other hand, looks like the proverbial class clown caught flatfooted on camera by the teacher—or is it the school's principal?—throwing spit-balls at his classmates in the middle of a pontifical lecture on

Einstein's Theory of Relativity. "I would rather take a swig of Scotch Whiskey," he seems to confide in the picture, "than chew on this elephant bone of bizarre geometrical abstractions."

That Chris Matthews had the rather lurid temerity to call his own president and commander-in-chief of the greatest army in the modern world "a jackass" and "an idiot," simply because Mr. Bush had deigned to reveal his putatively boyish side to media cameras, is rather sad and unfortunate. To be certain, it shows how pathologically superficial and emotionally bankrupt many of those who would have the unsuspecting public deem them to be gurus and witty interpreters of public opinion are in reality. There is a proverb among the Akan people which exhorts: "Watch whatever you say carefully, for anytime you point an accusing forefinger at an adversary, the other three fingers remind the accuser of his/her greater guilt.

26

Nile Valley Monopoly Revisited

The recent purported transformation of the erstwhile Organization of African Unity (OAU) into an African Union (AU), with supposedly more constructive political muscle, should ensure the total geopolitical, socioeconomic and cultural integration of the primeval continent. Indeed, it was in consonance with such agenda that on the eve of Ghana's independence in March 1957, President Kwame Nkrumah emphatically observed that: "The independence of Ghana is meaningless unless it is linked up with the total liberation of the African continent." No other premier had hitherto proffered such progressive and far-reaching commitment, even though by March 1957 at least six African countries, largely in the northern part of the continent, had been geopolitically emancipated. And it is this reason why the near-complete absence of Nkrumah's spirit at the maiden convocation of the African Union rendered the entire affair a little short of the climactic. It was almost as if the birthday anniversary of the United States was being celebrated without the ineluctable recognition of pioneering President, General George Washington. And to be certain, quite a number of writers, intellectuals and scholars who felt equally flabbergasted, such as this writer, have already written reams of rejoinders addressing this issue, thus facilitating our present need to spotlight other pressing questions.

The just-ended Ninth Conference on the Nile Basin, sponsored by the Uganda-based Nile Basin Initiative, purveyed prime cognitive grist or food for thought. At the conference Kenya's Dr. Raphael Kapiyo, dean of the faculty of environmental studies in that country's Maseno University, lamented the fact that in 1929 and, again, in 1959 agreements were signed by Britain and Italy, two notorious colonial imperialist powers, "awarding control of the Nile waters [exclusively] to Egypt" (**New York Beacon** 11/14-20/02: 10). In sum, these colonial powers decided that in order for Egypt to reap maximum economic benefits from the harnessing and utilization of the historic river, countries up-stream, and there are nine of them, could not equally maximize their use of the Nile much the same manner as Egypt could. In other words, based on their Eurocentric and racist understanding of Africa and its people, for Britain and Italy, the myth of Egypt as an extra-African civilization could be best preserved at the developmental expense of indigenous Africa.

What is surprising on the preceding score is less the fact that these bogus and noxious accords occurred at all, but the fact that it has taken almost two generations into the post-independence era for African scientists, leaders and intellectuals to seriously impeach their validity and consequently adopt a more salutary and organic or integral, revisionist approach. It is also tragic to learn from Nile Basin Initiative executive secretary Meraj Msuya that: "Among the 10 nations which form the Nile Basin, four are on the list of the poorest countries on the planet." Conversely, notes Burundian conference delegate Mathieu Nkurunziza, "More than any other country, Egypt has succeeded in developing a very productive irrigation system for its agriculture. However, up-stream, we're forbidden to use basin waters in order not to disturb the rational management of the Nile waters."

Needless to say, at the same time that these erstwhile colonial powers have virtually hamstrung and stymied the economic development of the so-called Black Africa, the latter's destroyers feign surprise at their victims' woeful inability to literally pull themselves by their proverbial shoe-strings.

The Egyptian response, unfortunately, has not been encouraging. For instance, Mustapha Abas, an Egyptian meteorological engineer and one of his country's delegates to the conference, riposted rather cavalierly that to question "Black Africa's" brazen economic massacre by Britain and Italy amounted to the "totally aberrant." Abas further trivialized matters by fatuously and disingenuously observing that while Egypt, indeed, benefited from the waters of the equatorial lakes that constituted the Nile, the latter's waters were, nevertheless, not "a decisive factor in the amount of water we use. Egypt has its own [decisive sources of] water supply—including its groundwater—which is not negligible." If the preceding, in fact, is the case, one wonders what Abas and the rest of the Egyptian delegation were about at the conference.

One thing, however, is certain: this dire crisis situation requires prompt remediation beyond what so far appears to amount merely to the sort of effete talk-shop which characterized the proceedings of the erstwhile Organization of African Unity. The veritable threats of drought and desertification necessitate the summary abrogation of the suicidal European compacts of 1929 and 1959. And the capricious and unmistakably nihilistic failure of the up-stream Nilotic countries to rectify this covenantal abomination may yet spell the doom of eastern Africa as we have known it over the past umpteen generations and centuries. U.

N. Secretary-General Kofi Annan must be prevailed upon to use his good offices, as it were, to remedy this cancerous dilemma. And here, it may also be significant to note that the trailblazing Ghanaian diplomat has played, and continues to play, a pivotal role in the salutary transformation of the continent from the pathological state of a neocolonial wooden model to an organic and functional civic polity.

The future of Africa can no longer be allowed to be determined by the gory whims of European imperialist ideologues. To borrow a philosophically pragmatist term from President Nkrumah, let all our actions and principles be guided, henceforth, by "Consciencism," the fundamentally rational realization of the progressive African personality. Africa must unite!

27

Ghana's Truth and Reconciliation Commission

Recently, the ruling New Patriotic Party (NPP) of Ghana borrowed a yellow-page from post-apartheid South Africa when President John Agyekum-Kufuor inaugurated a so-called National Reconciliation Commission. The latter organ has been accorded the mandate of "investigating abuses committed during the [tenure of] the five military [juntas] that ruled Ghana for a total of 22 years after the first coup in 1966" (Ghana.Com 5/9/02).

What makes the preceding event seem rather bizarre is that the very government initiating this process is a direct offshoot of the anti-Nkrumah political opposition that thunderously applauded Ghana's maiden coup in February 1966. It is also significant to recall that President Kufuor's mentor, the late Dr. Kofi Abrefa Busia, spearhead of the erstwhile Progress Party regime (1969–1972), served under the A. A. Afrifa- and Ankrah-led National Liberation Council (NLC) military junta that overthrew the Nkrumah regime. Under the guise of what some critics later described as an ethnocentric back-room deal, Dr. Busia served as national coordinator of a civic education campaign launched by the NLC shortly after the coup. Three years later, the Oxford-trained sociologist would be named Prime Minister, after a bitterly-fought election that some believe Mr. Komla Gbedemah, a cabinet member of Nkrumah's Convention People's Party (CPP) regime, had won.

Interestingly, Mr. Kufuor, also an Oxbridge graduate, would later proudly boast of having been the youngest cabinet member in the Progress Party government—he had been named Deputy Foreign Minister, under circumstances that even some of Mr. Kufuor's own closest associates have variously characterized as being tantamount to influence-peddling and outright nepotism. The preceding notwithstanding, it goes without saying that setting up the equivalent of a Truth and Reconciliation Commission implies that the initiator or institutionalizer pos-

116

sesses some tangible modicum of moral superiority over and above the measurable (or demonstrable) moral threshold of the targets or subjects of such a serious initiative. And this is why those of us who believe that the very establishment of a National Reconciliation Commission in Ghana reeks of fatuous plain-Jane hypocrisy and wanton wastage of scarce economic and human resources ought to be listened to; unless, of course, such a commission is being funded or underwritten by private sources.

But what is even more important to ask, at this juncture, is the simple question: What "truth" is there to learn that President John Agyekum-Kufuor is not already privy to? This question becomes very necessary because the substantive Ghanaian premier served for at least seven long-months under the extortionate military junta of former president Jerry John Rawlings' so-called Provisional National Defense Council (PNDC), the very junta which would proceed to stall electoral democracy in the country for nearly twenty years. The most articulate response that any staunch supporter of the NPP government has proffered in defense of President Kufuor's blatant nepotism is that all the government appointees who are known to be the latter's relatives—and to be certain, there are quite a number of them—are highly qualified for their jobs. And here, perhaps, it behooves every well-meaning student of Ghanaian politics to remind Mr. Kufuor and his minions that the science and art of governing a country is quite different from running one's family property. And one also dares to observe that almost any Ghanaian from a reputable and reasonably-enlightened family (or clan), and there are, literally, a legion, could assemble a remarkable cabinet for an administration almost wholly composed of that family (or clan). But, again, one may aptly ask: What would such a brazen move be saying about our sense of national identity as well as sociopolitical justice?

Some also claim that appointing his junior brother Minister of Defense is to ensure administrative security for the Kufuor presidency. A cursory glance at the administrative profiles of many past African dictatorships would easily convince the keen observer that Ghana may be dangerously poised on the cusp of another fledgling dictatorship, a "democratic" one, of course!

To be certain, appointing his pediatrician brother Minister of Health, for example, would not have seriously roiled any waters; rather, it would have been highly applauded. Sadly enough, however, some NPP stalwarts are wont to drawing vapid parallels between President Kufuor's appointment of Dr. Kwame Addo-Kufuor as Minister of Defense, and late President John F. Kennedy's appointment of his younger sibling, Robert F. Kennedy, as Attorney-General of the United States of America. This is rather amusing because, at the time of his appointment, one which many Americans of both parties did not take kindly to, by the way, Robert Kennedy had already distinguished himself as an active legal practitioner with quite an enviable civil rights track record.

A Truth and Reconciliation Commission can only be considered legitimate if its terms of reference include the thorough investigation of trans- or extra-military corruption at all levels of government in Ghana over the past 45 years. Mr. Rawlings' two terms of elective governance render him automatically immune from the dramaturgical circus of a National Reconciliation Commission. Ghanaians long ago reconciled themselves to the Rawlings phenomenon by twice choosing the former president, at the polls, over the NPP leadership. It is time to come to grips with realpolitik. Is anyone listening?

II

It was with acute regret and utter disappointment that I read Abdul-Rahman Alhassan's most recent report in the *African Abroad* of June 30, 2002. Titled, deadpan fashion, "Kufuor Tightens Security," the article discussed everything except what it proposed to discuss—i.e. national security in the post-Rawlings era. The foregoing assertion is poignantly borne out by the following abstract which appeared towards the end of Alhassan's rather brazen, if also morally reprehensible dissertation: "The Akan from which [sic] the president comes [hails?] have featured prominently in appointments to key [cabinet and other official] positions. This is seen as a major way of ensuring that adventurists do not have their way. After all, Rawlings ensured that Ewes held key positions. Although the nationality of his father remains a mystery, his [i.e. Rawlings'] mother comes from the Ewe ethnic group."

First of all, the preceding rather naively presumes that no Akans have been or can become political "adventurists," or coup plotters. Indeed, a cursory examination of stratocracies in Ghanaian political history points to the diametrically opposite direction. The writer also fails to highlight the fact that the resounding "success" of the Rawlings dictatorship was largely due to massive Akan support for the erstwhile (P)NDC regime. President Kufuor, who now self-righteously accuses Flt-Lt. Rawlings of obstreperous adventurist tendencies, was himself a staunch cabinet constable under the infamous Provisional National Defense Council.

Secondly, it does not pass muster to argue, as Abdul-Rahman Alhassan does in his article, that the antidote to perceived tribalism is counter-tribalism, instead of the unmitigable administration of justice and fair-play. At best what the preceding suggests is that the current government possesses no salutary leadership alternative to the status quo. At worst, the orchestrated and egregious practice of nepotism, and for that matter tribalism, is a vintage recipe for civic chaos, to speak less of a civil war. And, needless to say, God knows that "Government-By-Tit-For-Tat" is no sound strategy for nation-building. It did not work in Rwanda and Burundi and Liberia, and one hopes the staff of the so-called African Security Dialogue and Research Institute are taking good note of this fact.

As for such ad hominem epithet as: "Although the nationality of [Rawlings'] father remains a mystery, his mother comes from the Ewe ethnic group, the least said about it, the better. Indeed, it would be interesting to have some of Mr. Rawlings' detractors conduct a genealogical research into the paternity of the Ghanaian populace at large, including the researchers themselves, and present the rest of the world with an honest-to-God data and analyses of their findings. They may not like what they discover about themselves for themselves. Still, at this juncture, one makes bold to ask whether Abdul-Rahman Alhassan has assayed the basic journalistic tenet (or legwork) of learning from ex-President Rawlings whether the nationality of the latter's father has ever been "a mystery" to him. Needless to say, it is only the very height of arrogance that would prompt anybody to either question or impugn another's ancestral origins or nationality. Perhaps the writer ought to be reminded of the fact that Ghanaians constitutionally elected Mr. Rawlings twice without expressing any public qualms about the latter's paternity. And, also, need one venture to add that public knowledge of President Kufuor's paternity did not, sagaciously, deter the incumbent premier from serving under the "fatherless" Mr. Rawlings, or even protect President Kufuor from being accused of the far more flagrant charge of nepotism. To be certain, the science of good governance is more complex than the ability to locate one's agnatic or paternal provenance.

Thirdly, if one really wants to know how it came about that Ewes, who constitute roughly 16-percent of the country's population, dominated the Ghanaian military establishment, one only needs to read Ali A. Mazrui's quite formidable critique of African politics titled ***The Africans: A Triple Heritage*** (Boston: Little, Brown, 1986). In short, the under-representation of ethnic majorities in the coercive statal apparatus of the army is not unique or peculiar to Ghana. This anomaly has part of its origins in colonialism, the need of the European conquerors to "pacify" massive anti-imperialist and anti-colonial subjugation by aligning themselves with traditionally aggrieved, dominated and exploited ethnic minorities. The modern military as a hostile foreign instrument of repression thus did not appeal to powerful ethnic polities that saw no tangible reason to collaborate with their primary and mortal enemies against their own interests.

It is high time the Akan majority populace of Ghana stopped antagonizing and treating Ewes as total aliens or strangers from Jupiter, or some such planet. Indeed, many of us who are of "high" Akan royal backgrounds also have equally "high" Ewe royal ancestry. And while the intent here is not to apotheosize or hagiographize the Ewe, or any other perceived Ghanaian minority group, for that matter, the road to national unity and prosperity rests squarely with leaders of ethnic and cultural majority groups. Whoever contemptuously labeled the Ewe "Number Nine," meaning ghetto Ghanaians, must be ashamed of themselves. The interesting aspect of it all is that here we are, in the United States, decrying the soul-withering pathology of racism, even as some of our kinsmen vigorously propose counter-tribalism as a blueprint to national development. God save us from ourselves!

28

Wonders of the Libero-African World

Recent news reports originating from Monrovia, Liberia, speak of a press conference called by that eventful country's president, Charles Taylor, during which the latter announced to his country and the world at large that his excellency intended to embark on the primitive cultural practice of male polygamy (or more appropriately *polygyny*), in the name of traditional African cultural heritage. Taylor is further quoted as saying that Liberian tradition enjoins his statutorily recognized wife and the country's first lady, Jewel Howard, "to fish for a woman and bring her over to him."

Indeed, what is most nauseating about the foregoing, assuming its veracity, inheres in the fact that it patently reduces the hydra-headed problems of the hitherto war-torn country to one of the phallic or pudendal obsession of an apparent psychiatric basket case parading in the name of a legitimate leader. Rather than demonstrating his manhood, or virility, through passionate engagement in such constructive and positively far-reaching projects as education, health and economic development, it seems that Mr. Taylor has opted for the proverbial primrose path of Hobbesian bestiality. And to call, of all convocations, a press conference just to make such a fatuous announcement is all the more disturbing.

Indeed, when the Liberian strongman states: "I have no intention of insulting my people. I will fulfill my traditional requirements [obligations?] in [to?] this country," he achieves precisely the diametrically opposite. Perhaps the "jungle-war" veteran imagines himself to be living in the early nineteenth century, during which period his countrymen and women were, ironically, even far more intelligent than this veritable intellectual elf would have the rest of us believe. To be certain, one would have thought that Mr. Taylor by now would be passionately engaged in revamping his sullied image as a convicted criminal and a marauding terrorist; instead, he has the proverbial international community confirming what

121

many of us have been suspecting all along—that this man is a vintage moral reprobate pretending to champion the cause of justice and responsible leadership. On this score, Taylor is essentially no better than the infamous Master-Sergeant Samuel Doe. Indeed, it would be quite apt to describe these two rascals as a cut of the same fabric.

Needless to say, Dr. Mohamed Ibn Chambas and his ECOWAS Secretariat may need to convene an emergency summit of West African leaders to discuss President Taylor's latest manifestation of clinical madness, and also craft and implement a moral code of presidential conduct for all constitutionally elected premiers of the sub-region to observe. For not only is the Liberian chieftain a gross embarrassment to West Africa, as a whole, but he is also a veritable threat to our moral, intellectual and cultural development. Indeed, as long as Mr. Taylor kept his lecherous tendencies to himself, they were squarely a domestic issue; now that he has called a press conference to announce it to the rest of the world, they have become a national and regional security issue. Needless to say, such reprehensible behavior offers very bad role-modeling to Liberia's adult-male population, particularly when the substantive commander-in-chief cavalierly offers the equally opprobrious peccadilloes of his predecessors as legitimate conjugal precedents. The Butcher of Monrovia is, for instance, quoted as making the following rather cynical statement: "Pastor William R. Tolbert dowried women in this country. In fact, some of his women are in town asking me for assistance" (*African Abroad* 10/31/02: 6). If, indeed, he were that intelligent, the foregoing quote would have taught Mr. Taylor something about the villainy of his chosen course of pathological, conjugal fulfillment.

Perhaps, it is also important to remind the Liberian chief constable that if he were that serious about toeing the time-tested traditions of African culture, he would have begun with a name change. Needless to say, in African tradition and culture one's name embodies one's ethos and axiological orientation. But, perhaps even more significantly, Taylor needs to be reminded that his brand or species of presidency has no organic basis in traditional African culture: it is largely a Western adaptation, one that was summarily imposed, in some glaring instances. And while slavo-colonial multi-nationalism has virtually indigenized this political regime, it must be squarely envisaged as an administrative mode of sheer convenience. In short, unless Mr. Taylor could trace his lineage through an indigenous Liberian royal family, his fatuous assay at conjugal primitivism is simply the pathetic and psychotic act of an ideological nihilist.

Then again, Taylor could, perhaps, make the patently reasonable case that having slaughtered the husbands and boyfriends, or lovers, of so many Liberian women, the only way the he can think of making amends is to marry and take care of the legion bereaved. But, here again, whether these women would consent to licensed coitus with the very murderer of their significant others, as it were, is wholly a different story altogether. Indeed, it is a pity, if not an outright tragedy, that a country that once prided itself with being the lodestar of African modernism should be summarily reduced to the level of one sick man's libido. May God save us from the enemy within, even as we battle the equally insidious forces of ideological and cultural imperialism. For, let us make no mistake, this "**Taylorian pathology**" or "**Tayloriasis,**" as a colleague prefers to characterize it, is more widespread than many of us would like to believe. Indeed, Mr. Taylor's madness quite epitomizes the grueling crisis of identity that has become characteristic of continental Africa's post-colonial era, Liberia's somewhat unique evolution notwithstanding.

29

A Nuke Agenda for Africa

Raging global events regarding India-Pakistan, Afghanistan and North Korea, point to the grim fact that the language of Washington, particularly Washington under the Bush-Cheney administration, is one of brazen nuclear brinkmanship or "nuke-politics," the latest synonym for the geopolitical concept of "realpolitik." Thus while Mr. Bush has been swift and prompt in responding to "crises" provoked by the preceding Third World countries, our Republican president has been totally dismissive and, at best, glancingly patronizing in his attitude towards African affairs. Recently, for instance, just when many of us—ardent and avid students of American foreign policy—were beginning to sigh with a tad relief that His Excellency was finally beginning to act like the responsible global leader that his administration vociferously claims to be, Mr. Bush abruptly pulled the plugs on his then-intended business tour of the primal continent. (The White House on January 20 put out an official notice stating that the President's scuttled African confab would now take place in Nigeria sometime in July or August).

Not that many of us had any serious reason to take the President up on his word; it was simply to respectfully accord him the proverbial benefit of the doubt. And then, just as we had suspected all along, the White House issued a bland statement claiming that the latter's long-running saber-rattling with President Saddam Hussein, of Iraq, demanded more immediate attention than Mr. Bush's rendezvous with Africa.

It goes without saying that outside of Afghanistan and, perhaps, our metaphorical Big Apple, the African continent has innocently and silently suffered more of the tragic and psychically devastating consequences of America's so-called war on terrorism than any other spot on the globe. And here, the singular allusion is to the august East African polities of Kenya and Tanzania. Of course, the depressing fact that the continent is woefully besieged by hundreds of thousands of millions of Aids cases, which threaten to unleash an unprecedented state of acute depopulation, since the apocalyptic experience of the infamous trade in African humanity, must constitute an exigent or imperative need for a presidential tour of duty. In the bizarre imagination of the White House, it seems, the mere and largely unproven allegation that Mr. Hussein might be hiding some caches of "weapons of mass destruction," whatever that protean phrase means, supersedes any moral claims of Africa to the beneficent attention or audience of the United States.

Imagine, however, a hypothetical case scenario whereby South Africa, Egypt, Ghana, Nigeria or Libya came out publicly tomorrow and claimed to be in possession of nuclear warheads and actually threatened to use of proliferate them, unless Washington promptly succored to our myriad socioeconomic needs. Would the White House then stay put as it is behaving presently? Indeed, CNN's Miles O'Brien (1/3/03) put it best when the often witty news-anchor alluded to the glaring fact that the Bush administration seemed to be all too willing to talk serious business with only those countries which possessed nuclear weapons capability, thus counterproductively making it seem rather attractive to go nuke, if only to use such lethal technology as a bargaining blue-chip.

To some people, the preceding scenario may sound like a putrid joke; but let no one be mistaken: The domestic policies of the Bush II administration over the past twenty-four months testify to the veracity of such contingency. Almost every significant economic package unwrapped by the current administration has been a virtual bonanza for the filthily rich and powerful, whom Mr. Bush seems to envisage as *the real Americans*. In fact, during the heat of his presidential campaign, when challenged on his humongous tax giveaways for corporate moguls, the then-candidate Bush's most rational riposte was to sneer that the rich and powerful would receive the lion's share of his tax largesse because the latter also paid most of the taxes. Thus in his scale of values, the responsible leadership concept of *noblesse oblige* or *charity* is non-existent. Maybe if somebody told Mr. Bush that if his excellency deigned to be a little kindly and charitable towards those of us deemed virtual nonentities, our chief constable's purported linguistic solecism could be felicitously meliorated.

Needless to say, the preceding points to the fact that our supreme commander seems to lack any sympathy for the proverbial "wretched of the earth"—apologies to Frantz Fanon. On January 4, 2003, for instance, the President was reported by CNN to have verbally reached out to newly-elected Kenyan president Mwai Kibaki and promised to be forthcoming with any means that would facilitate the smooth-running of Mr. Kibaki's terror-ridden, debt and corruption-wracked country of some 38 million-plus Africans. Indeed, we wish we could be cheerful about such indubitably glad tidings; alas, we simply cannot, at least not until such promise is shown to possess the stinging peck of our bald eagle.

Of course, suggesting that Africans embark on a nuclear weapons program on an increasingly dangerous global landscape sounds patently puerile and indeflectibly flaky. However, under the foregoing circumstances who said we, really, have anything to lose? Indeed, the only obstacles to the constructive acquisition of such potent mainstream global vocabulary are economic strictures. Needless to say, Africans have more than our fair share of highly-trained scientists, scattered all over the world, to undertake such a manly and noble project. Obviously, we cannot go at it individually, and so the best approach would be one of collaboration among such potential nuclear powers as South Africa, Ghana, Congo and Egypt. And by all means, should the necessity arise, let us call on potential allies like North Korea, and who knows who else…. For, in the final analysis, is not the saying valid that: "What is good for the goose, is also good for the gander?"

Several decades ago, pioneering and immortalized Ghanaian president Kwame Nkrumah asserted the following during the heat of his country's struggle for "self-re-governance": "We prefer self-government with danger to servitude in tranquillity." Africans would do well to heed this immutable call; unlike Baghdad, however, we have no need to embark on our nuke program sub rosa. For as a socio-economically and politically cannibalized people, what need is there to fear that which we have collectively already experienced over the last 500 years?

Indeed, for many Africans and African-Americans, President Bush and Senator Trent Lott are a cut of the same cloth. To be certain, there is only a slight difference between these two Southern white men. The latter seems to be more obtuse in publicly preaching racial animosity and segregation, whereas the more clever Mr. Bush silently but resolutely practices the same. For His Excellency, there seems to be ample justification in blaming the poor, destitute and powerless for being too dumb and shiftless to amass tax-free wealth and pelf. For Mr. Lott, on the other hand, sheer **Blackness** is worthy of blame.

30

A Clash of Cultural Values

The problem of acute cultural disorientation continues to raise serious concerns among many members of the continental African community resident here in the United States. Oftentimes, the problem appears to be more familial than individual; it has more to do with parenting than whether or not one feels secure and comfortable with the cultural values and mores of the voluntarily adopted new country. The difficulty stems from the fact that oftentimes the decision of some continental African parents to become permanent residents, or even citizens, of America is not logically matched by a carefully considered appreciation of the fact that citizenship in any polity ineluctably implies unreserved acceptance of the cultural values of the chosen polity. Consequently, many Africans who have been resident in this country for a decade or more, and who have become mothers and fathers of American-born children persist in falsely convincing themselves that, contrary to empirical realities, both of these immigrant parents and their native-born children are bona fide citizens of continental Africa.

Several factors are responsible for such paralogical state of affairs. The first and, perhaps, most significant factor is the stark and unsavory reality of diasporic African maltreatment by mainstream society. In their countries of birth, many of these parents had hailed from major ethnic groups which dominated and, in many instances, dictated the terms of the collective national destiny at the socio-political, cultural and economic levels. In sum, these African-born parents had shared the prevailing national prejudice. Once in America, however, they soon discover to their utter horror and chagrin that they are no longer in the mainstream of national prejudice. One knee-jerk response has been for some of these parents to stridently differentiate themselves from members of the African-American community. This tack, or approach, is often catalyzed by cunning and divisive white-Americans who, viscerally fearing that the certain political unification of African-Americans with their continental African brethren implies the logical doom of Aryan supremacy (for many of the negative stereotypes traditionally associated with diasporic Africans, are found, forthwith, to be incongruent with the latter African group's general cognitive orientation and socio-political and cultural experiences), coddle and hoodwink continental Africans into falsely assuming a superior stance towards their diasporic relatives. In some instances, this centrifugal ploy succeeds; ultimately, however, the primary beneficiary is the white-American detractor who, invariably, comes to despise both African sub-groups. The preceding, in effect, constitutes much of the pathetic global image of the African, both in the proverbial Motherland and the diaspora.

The other tack, which is equally superficial, if also because it is purely reactionary, is what this writer has labeled *Dashiki Afrocentrism*. Any continental African afflicted with the latter disease invariably pretends that even though s/he is resident in the United States, s/he is immutably a continental African. As parents, this category of Africans insist that its moral and cultural values are impregnable, or simply the best in the world. It is, therefore, only too logical and rational to unreservedly reject American moral and cultural values, be they mainstream and Eurocentric or marginal and diasporic.

Inwardly, the *Dashiki Afrocentrist* envies European-Americans for their apparently absolute domination of state-of-art technology and all that passes for modernity. This is not entirely his/her fault; for, during the colonial era, the *Dashiki Afrocentrist* had been indoctrinated, in the name of education and scientific scholarship, to accept inferiority as part of his/her manifest destiny. And even though two generations of post-colonial self-governance and phenomenal developments in high-end scientific research attest to the indelible fact of the global African having invented both modern technology and civilization, so corrosive has the damage been that his blustering and reactionary public rhetoric of superiority notwithstanding, the continental African never quite negotiated the epic trauma of imposed and perennially enforced culture of inferiority. Indeed, some diasporic Africans are also afflicted with *Dashiki Afrocentrism*, a paradoxical situation that causes them to both identify with and despise their continental brethren at the same time. For present purposes, however, the latter canker would be reserved and taken up for further disquisition at a later date.

The preceding discussion is in reference to an article that appeared in the *West African News'* edition of December 15, 2002. The latter is a freely circulated continental African community newspaper. Titled "The Tragedy of a Nigerian Family," the article retailed the harrowing story of a couple whose four children were literally snatched from them and callously masticated by the juggernaut that is the New York City foster care system. It appears the article in question was at least a second installment run by *West African News*; and since several significant details are missing, this writer is, perforce, limited to a telling quotation from the father of the children, three of whom are now in their twenties, and the youngest allegedly felled by the bullets of a neighborhood thug. Among other remarks, Mr. Olu Abidekun makes the following charge against New York City's Administration for Children's Services: "We have been treated as if we are not human beings. They have destroyed our family. The children have been grossly abused. This is an appeal to the African Community to help stop the bastardization of our culture."

It is interesting to recall that in the ***West African News***' article, the Abidekuns are accused of having maltreated their "lost" children. And although the children were alienated from their parents for some 14 years, the Nigerian Consulate in New York City, the most appropriate institution of recourse or redress for the Abidekuns, flatly denies ever being informed or contacted all this while about the couple's ordeal. One thing, though, is certain: There is no uniformed African culture; and what is more, we do not exactly know which aspects of Mr. Abidekun's culture is purportedly being "bastardized" by American society, for which the couple seeks urgent redress from "the African Community." If this, indeed, happens to be raw and naked parental tyranny, as the Administration of Children's Services maintains, then, by all means, let the Abidekuns count out those of us who are dead-set against corporal punishment in the specious name of "discipline" from their rather protean designation and definition of "the African Community." For the patently evil act of tyranny transcends both culture and nationality.

THE END

About the Author

Winner of the 1988 John J. Reyne Artistic Achievement Award for English Poetry at New York City College, where he earned his bachelor's degree (summa cum laude) in English, Journalism and African-American Studies, Kwame Okoampa-Ahoofe, Jr. was born and raised in Ghana. He has also been a Ford Foundation Undergraduate Fellow in the English Department of City College (1987–1990), where he also served as Editorial Writer and Opinions Editor for *The Campus*, the main student newspaper. The 1999 winner of the Best Essay Award by *Nassau Review* for his essay "When Human Dignity is Besieged: An Afrocentric Critique of the Diary of Anne Frank," an essay that made controversial headlines in the *Letters* column of the *New York Times*, Okoampa-Ahoofe is the author of *Dorkordicky Ponkorhythms*(1997), *Atumpan*(1998) and *Obaasima*(2000), all of them collections of poetry. His poetry has also been featured in *Downtown*. Earlier on, his poems were performed on Ghana's national radio and television, as well as the country's major national cultural centers. Presently, he teaches English and Journalism at Nassau Community College of the State University of New York, Garden City. Okoampa-Ahoofe has also taught African and African-American history and culture at Indiana State University, Terre Haute, and Mercy College at Dobbs Ferry, New York. A graduate with master's and doctoral degrees from Temple University, Philadelphia, Okoampa-Ahoofe is a leading opinion columnist for *The New York Beacon*, having also written book reviews and news articles for *The New York Amsterdam News* for fifteen years. He also writes regular political commentary for the bi-weekly newspaper *African Abroad*.

0-595-32678-1

www.ingramcontent.com/pod-product-compliance
Lightning Source LLC
Chambersburg PA
CBHW020237290526
45784CB00003B/1007